Seize

the

Day

Seven Steps to Achieving the
Extraordinary in an Ordinary World

Seize the Day

Seven Steps to Achieving the Extraordinary in an Ordinary World

By
Danny Cox and John Hoover

Seize the Day: 7 Steps to Achieving the Extraordinary in an Ordinary Life

ISBN 81-8274-203-X

First Indian Edition: 2006

© Danny Cox and John Hoover

Original English Edition published by **Career Press**, Inc., 3 Tice Road, PO Box 687, Franklin Lakes, NJ 07417. Indian Edition published in arrangement by Pentagon Press.

Management Update 24x7(An imprint)

Corporate office
A-38 Hauz Khas
New Delhi-110016
Ph. 41517091, 41656996, 7, 8
Fax: 41656997
Email: pentagonpress@touchtelindia.net

Sales office
105-106, 4262, St. #3
Ansari Road, Darya Ganj
Website: www.pentagon-press.com

Printed at Thomson Press (P) Ltd., New Delhi

This edition is for sale in Indian Subcontinent only

Dedication/Introduction

Of the many mentors who have helped me "seize the day," I dedicate this to three standouts.

The first is Virgil Cox, my coal-miner father. Out of his meager earnings he figured out a way to obtain his private pilot's license. On one of those great Sunday afternoon flights out of the Marion, Illinois airport, he let me fly an airplane for the first time. I was 12 years old. With his unceasing encouragement I progressed from that 90 mph airplane to flying supersonic fighters at 20 miles per minute (1,200 mph). It was quite an adventure.

The second mentor is Mike Vance, founder and former dean of Disney University where he had also headed up the Idea and People Development Department for Walt Disney. When I heard him speak there in Anaheim I was at a low point in my life. I had just destroyed my employer's top office because I was so bad as a manager. That day I learned people skills that really worked and this profound bit of philosophy:

"We do what we are. We are what we think. What we think is determined by what we learn. What we learn is determined by what we experience and what we experience is determined by what we expose ourselves to and what we do with that experience."

That half-day seminar of Mike's was the turning point in my rebuilding that office into an industry leader.

The third mentor is easily the most interesting person I have ever known. His name was Jim Newton and he was author of *Uncommon Friends,* which chronicles his close friendships with Thomas Edison,

Henry Ford, Harvey Firestone, Charles Lindbergh, and Nobel Prize winner, Dr. Alexis Carrel. He taught me that his great friends had three things in common:

1. A sense of destiny.
2. A spirit of adventure.
3. A capacity for growth.

In 1999, at the age of 94, Jim left this realm. Even in that last year he was still telling people, in his characteristically humorous way, "I can't say much for my past, but my future is spotless."

As you can see from the loving encouragement of a blue-collar father, to Mickey Mouse, to Thomas Edison, it's been quite a ride—and its not over yet.

"The best is yet to be."

Contents

Foreword

I've spent a professional lifetime seeking out the potential in people. To me, people represent endless possibilities. Within each individual there is tremendous power waiting to be unleashed. I've found nothing more gratifying in my career than to see a man or a woman finally *come into his or her own*. People, possibilities, power: These are among the topics that have inspired me to write scores of books and preach thousands of sermons over the years.

Through those years, I've learned firsthand how it's possible for anyone with a big enough heart to accomplish unbelievable results. The size of your pocketbook, your physical stature, and your formal schooling mean very little when it comes to long-term success. It's the ability to place oneself in the future, plan, and execute faithfully that makes all the difference. Where the power of human potential is concerned, the sky's the limit.

That's why I'm proud of my good friend Danny Cox. I've watched his career grow. I know what a rich blessing *his* speaking and writing have been to so many people across this great country. Now, Danny has topped himself once again. This time he's carved out a seven-step, *high-performance process* that will make the most of your natural abilities, education and experience. Danny weaves an entertaining and informative fabric out of his executive experiences, Air Force test pilot escapades and Ozark country common sense. As usual, he communicates it all in the warm, easygoing, amusing style that's become his trademark on the speaker's platform. Tapping your reservoir of personal potential has never been explained more clearly. Following Danny's time-proven formula will truly enable you to *Seize The Day*.

—Dr. Robert H. Schuller

Seize
the
Day

Seven Steps to Achieving the
Extraordinary in an Ordinary World

The High-Performance Process

Performance is Personal

"People are always blaming their circumstances for what they are. I don't believe in circumstances. The people who get on in this world are the people who get up and look for the circumstances they want, and, if they can't find them, make them."

—George Bernard Shaw

Some of my happiest college days were spent spelunking. I mapped many a cave for the geology department at Southern Illinois University. What might look to most people like a pile of rocks in the middle of an Illinois pasture can also be the entrance to an underground adventure.

And so it was that three friends and I slid on our stomachs through a narrow crevice and discovered a sizable underground cavern. Following the beams of our flashlights, we ventured deeper into the cave until we came to a ledge. Using the rope we had brought with us, we lowered ourselves down 15 feet or so to the next level.

After exploring a while longer, we decided to head back. When we came to the rope draped over the ledge, we discovered that the moisture in the cave had made it wet and slippery. No matter how hard we tried, none of us could secure a tight enough grip to climb up. As we enthusiastically set out on our adventure earlier that day, we had ignored some of the details that now loomed menacingly before us.

For starters, nobody knew where we were. We hadn't bothered to tell anyone that we were going to explore a specific cave in a specific place. We just sort of stumbled on to the entrance. There was no prominent opening at the mouth of the cave, only a narrow 18-inch gap in a pile of rocks in the middle of a pasture. We were probably the only human beings alive who were aware that this cave existed.

Our flashlights were getting dim and the air was getting stale. With the urgency of our situation beginning to increase the tension among us, we discussed our options. There didn't seem to be any obvious solution. We weren't aware that we were holding ourselves back with conventional thinking. Our mistake was looking for the *obvious*.

It wasn't until we turned our flashlights off to save the batteries that I began to see possibilities that we hadn't previously considered. In the darkness of the underground cavern, I noticed that the small pieces of driftwood scattered around us were *glowing*. While relying on the beams from our flashlights to illuminate our way, we hadn't noticed the phosphorous properties of the fungus-covered logs that made them glow in the dark.

The glow from the rocks didn't assist us in any practical way. What it did was prick my creativity enough to realize that the solution to our problem was probably close at hand if only we could look at our situation differently. The glowing driftwood made me feel as if the answer had to be there and we just weren't seeing it. As it turned out, I went back to the rope that was too slippery to grip with our hands and realized we might be better off using our *feet*. We tied loops in the rope and climbed up the sheer face of the ledge using the rope as a makeshift ladder.

Different eyes

The necessity for, and the rewards that flow from, a commitment to personal high performance aren't always obvious. Unless we can mentally switch off the lights and study the glow around us, we probably won't appreciate how important our role is in the scheme of life. In a nutshell, who we are and how we glow in our private lives determines who we are in our professional lives. We just need to sit quietly in the dark long enough to see how we glow. It's in the darkness that our true character shines the brightest.

I've found it universally true that an individual with a high sense of personal ethics and integrity in his or her professional life will have the same ethics and integrity in his or her personal life. The same holds true of enthusiasm, drive, goals, and general initiative. Once committed to the *high-performance process,* high-performance people are *always* high-performance people, lights on or lights off.

Different people may demonstrate their performance in different ways, but, in the end, high performance is a way of life. The difference between a high-performance person and a potential high-performance person is the decision to look at life through different eyes and to invest the effort necessary to become a person who makes his or her own circumstances.

Performance is everyone's business

The primary thesis of my previous book, *Leadership When the Heat's On,* simply states that *no organization can rise above the quality of its leadership.* That's a valuable idea to hang on the wall opposite your desk at the office, post on your bathroom mirror at home, or tattoo on the back of your hand. Some folks miss the point and agree wholeheartedly that leadership is the cause of all their ills. Unfortunately, these people are looking for somewhere else to place the responsibility for their circumstances and aren't accepting their own role in leadership, no matter how obscure.

Everybody is his or her *own* leader, plain and simple. Every person within an organization plays a role in leadership. An organization is a *system.* In a system, the performance of each component has an effect on the performance of the organization as a whole. If you work alone, your commitment to personal high performance will have a more profound impact on your success than the commitment of a single individual at General Motors.

Whether or not you work alone or work for the world's worst boss in a large organization, a personal commitment to high performance influences your circumstances. The greater your commitment to personal high performance, the better the circumstances for you *and* everyone in the organization. Whatever the leaders believe and practice will be reflected throughout the entire organization. *Your* beliefs and values will be reflected in your *performance.*

Nevertheless, the success or failure of individuals within an organization depends largely upon each person's willingness to adopt the vision and commitment of the organization's leadership. One of the primary challenges of leadership is to market its vision to the individuals in the organization and entice them to embrace the vision as their own. At the same time, influence runs the other direction. You might not be the leader, but that doesn't mean leadership isn't important to you.

As individuals within organizations, we all have a professional obligation to keep our leaders honest and focused by working diligently to produce results that reflect leadership's vision. The success of your role in the system is a direct reflection of your commitment to personal high performance.

Give and take

Dedication to personal high performance requires a healthy ability to give selflessly to others and to receive gratefully the rewards of a job well done. Giving and receiving go hand in hand. While it's true that our motivation for giving is not to create indebtedness in others, someone who gives all and accepts nothing in return is fulfilling some sacrificial need in his or her personal agenda.

Conversely, people who want everything given to them without investing something of themselves are seeking a return to infancy and a nurturing, all-providing parent. Either way, what's missing is the balance between giving and receiving that's necessary for a fulfilled life. Even if you work alone at homemaking and/or philanthropy, you will benefit as much or more from a commitment to personal high performance as someone within a large organization. The cornerstone of personal high performance in both cases is to help others and to accept their help in return.

Happy campers, high flyers

The quest for personal high performance can become an ongoing journey and is never an end in itself. The pursuit of personal high performance is the source of tremendous pleasure and gratification. It's the feeling an athlete experiences in victory, the sensation an actor feels during a standing ovation, the satisfaction an artist experiences when his or her music, painting, or sculpture makes the statement it was intended to make.

For me, it's the way I felt when I broke the sound barrier for the very first of what eventually became almost 2000 times during my years as an Air Force test pilot and air show pilot. Even though Chuck Yeager had been the first person to break the sound barrier 11 years earlier in an aircraft designed for supersonic flight, my first supersonic experience was unforgettable.

I was alone at the controls of an F-86D fighter, in a vertical dive at 45,000 feet, full throttle, with my afterburner lit, watching the Okefenoke Swamp rapidly approaching my windshield. In an aircraft not built for supersonic speeds, some strange things began to happen. Being a test pilot, I was supposed to observe all phenomenon calmly and objectively. However, when the wings on the jet began to twist and bend slightly under the pressure, my eyes got a little wider.

I heard creaks and groans from the aircraft's framework that I'd never heard before. Then I "punched through" and the feeling was unbelievable. Not so much because I'd broken through the sound barrier, but because I could now plant my feet firmly on the console and yank back on the stick to pull out of my nose dive. What a *thrill!*

The *high-performance process* is not about winning or being number one. It's about running the good race and pursuing a personal best. However, life is a series of ups and downs. No one lives on a perpetual high (although some work hard at maintaining a perpetual low). Anyone determined to focus on negativity has an addiction to life-strangling habits that block personal productivity.

Those with a solid grip on reality accept that times are sometimes tough and results often fall short of expectations. That's okay to a

high-performance person. High-performance people don't congratu-
late themselves for just taking a stab at something. Making an effort is
not on face value worthy of reward. When a person makes the best
effort s/he is capable of making, rewards are due—whether or not the
goal is achieved. Too often, too many folks settle for too little effort.
Never the high-performance person who is "on the grow "

Natural vs. self-imposed barriers

To best illustrate what personal high performance is, it's important to first understand where and how all of us tend to fall short of
our potential. Self-imposed barriers take over where natural barriers
leave off. Most people never know the difference between the two
and, therefore, erroneously assume that their lack of achievement is
someone else's fault.

Self-imposed barriers get higher and wider when individuals focus
on their own weaknesses as pointed out to them by friends, employ-
ers, teachers, parents, conventional wisdom, etc. Shifting focus to
developing strengths immediately weakens self-imposed barriers.

An example of a *natural* barrier is my career in the NBA. I have
no career in the National Basketball Association and I have no reason
to be ashamed of my inability to play professional basketball in the
United States. At 5'5" and 50-plus years of age, there is a natural
barrier between my abilities and the job requirements of guarding
Michael Jordan. Even those few 5'6" miracle players who *do* play
professional basketball will be retired long before they're 50.

Physical challenges are the most obvious of the natural barriers
and it's important to be realistic about them. Mental challenges are
more insidious and less well-defined. In most cases where someone is
not performing up to his or her ability, it's a direct result of a self-
imposed psychological barrier. A self-imposed barrier is not a wall in
life, it's simply the *margin* where nothing has yet been written—yet.

If you're frustrated and wonder why you aren't getting any further in life, you're undoubtedly looking at that margin as if it were a
wall. Many people feel as if they've *maxed-out* and simply can't do any
more or any better than they've done to date. Most of us get our cues
from our parents and feel deep inside that we can't rise any further

Where You Are Now

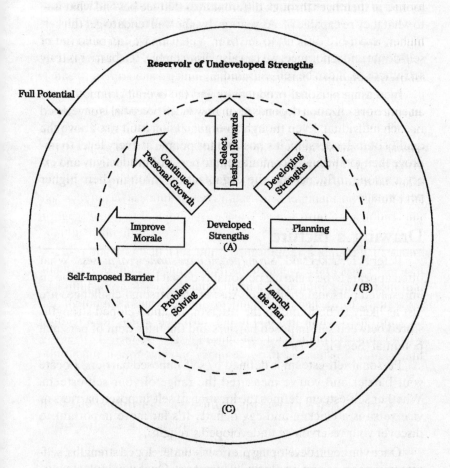

Figure 0.1

Developed strengths (A) are inside Self-Imposed Barriers (B).
Your personal revevoir of Underdeveloped Strengths (C) resides
outside of your Self-Imposed Barriers.

professionally, make any more money or perform at a higher level than our parents did. Until we make a more informed decision of our own, that is.

Such people haven't seen themselves glow in the dark. They haven't looked at their lives through different eyes that see beyond what is—to what they're capable of. As years go by, the wall tends to get thicker, higher, and more difficult to see over. Yet, what we can build out of self-doubt and ignorance, we can also disassemble. If a barrier is truly self-imposed, it can be self-deposed.

Increasing personal productivity and the overall productivity of an entire organization depends upon how much potential is developed in each individual. Even though an organization can't rise above the quality of its leadership, it's possible for people at every level to improve their lot through a commitment to personal productivity and exert a strong influence on the organization through their higher performance.

Drawing a picture

Peter F. Drucker said *"Strong people have strong weaknesses."* What often appears to be a glaring personality deficit is more likely to be an unresolved personal challenge. Answers to personal challenges are just as likely to be found in the reservoir of undeveloped strengths stored between self-imposed barriers and the full extent of personal potential (See Fig. 0-1).

Personal self-esteem is defined by self-imposed barriers. Locate your barrier and you've measured the range of your self-esteem. Whether self-esteem defines the location of self-imposed barriers or vice versa is a chicken-and-egg debate. It's far more important to discover your reservoir of undeveloped strengths.

Once you begin developing previously undeveloped strengths, self-esteem improves and productivity increases. Once you look at yourself through different eyes and see your undeveloped strengths, full of promise and potential, you can't help but become more enthusiastic. In the same manner, leaders who are responsible for the development of others need to see members of the organization not only for what

Your Thermometer of Personal Potential

Figure 0.2

Where You Want To Be

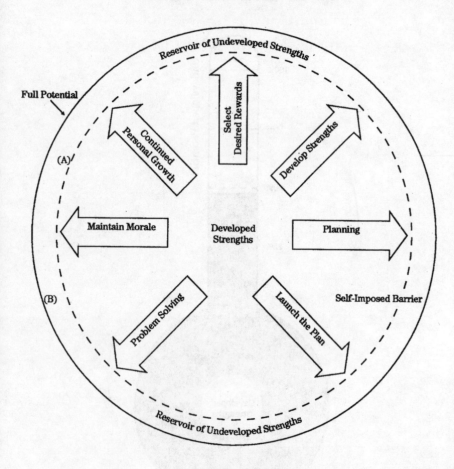

Figure 0.3

As you execute the seven steps of the high-performance process, Self-Imposed Barriers (A) are pushed back as Undeveloped Strengths become Developed Strengths and you edge increasingly closer to your Full Potential (B).

they have accomplished in the past, but also in light of their undeveloped strengths.

Another way to illustrate the difference between developed and undeveloped potential is to visualize a thermometer (See Fig. 0-2). The mercury level represents your current level of developed potential. The top of the thermometer represents the full range of your potential. The exercise involves identifying and resolving the issues that cause the mercury level to stay below what you're capable of.

How likely you are to achieve your full potential depends upon how hot or cold you're running. Obviously, whatever fires your boilers becomes the key ingredient to fuel the development of undeveloped strengths. Ask yourself:

"Where do I see myself on my thermometer?"

"Where do I want to be on the thermometer next year?"

"What's my action plan for getting there?"

7 steps of the high-performance process

The following chapters are devoted to methods and techniques of expanding the circle of self-imposed barriers as more and more strengths are developed. As undeveloped strengths are developed through the *high-performance process* (See Fig. 0-3), personal performance increases and life changes. The heat that causes the mercury to rise in the personal potential thermometer comes from the same energy source that heats the center of the circle of self-imposed barriers.

Think of the arrows that push the circle of self-imposed barriers outward as radiating heat. The heat is produced by burning desire. The desire to earn more, to live and work happier, to accomplish more meaningful tasks, and/or to achieve a more desirable lifestyle are just a few examples of fuel for the fire. The desire to live and work differently is different for every person. The business leader will raise the overall productivity of the organization as s/he helps individuals to push back their circles of self-imposed barriers.

The critical element is a desire to improve personal performance in the first place. It's a deep-seated yearning to break your own barriers, to push into the unknown territory of your own undeveloped strengths. It's a scary thought. Someone with no innate desire to increase personal productivity will tire of this book quickly. The assumption throughout the seven-step *high-performance process* is that something new is called for. Whether change is a personal challenge or a professional responsibility, the process must be fueled with personal desire.

It's also essential to work on all seven steps. Working on one or only a selected few will not result in lasting improvements in personal performance. As the circle of self-imposed barriers is pushed back, there needs to be a balance in the effort you exert in all seven areas. Once you commit to the *high-performance process,* all seven areas need to be revisited regularly to keep the process moving.

Performance anxiety

Some people are hot and some people are cold. The difference is desire. Observing a person's lifestyle and appetite for life is the easiest way to take his or her temperature. More than anything else, *growing confidence* is the most visible evidence of a hot personality. It's easy to sense whether someone is focused on personal high performance. His or her behavior and attitude toward self, others and the circumstances, will reflect the necessary personal commitment.

Nobody can see the future any clearer than the next person. However, the high-performance person is excited about the potential of the future just the same. The lukewarm or cold personality would rather stay wrapped in the comfort of the familiar. Change means uncertainty and uncertainty can cut both ways. Although the new lifestyle might be better, chances are that it might be worse. Hence the strong affinity for the familiar.

One of the primary reasons people *avoid* developing their previously undeveloped strengths is fear of the imminent life changes that an increase in personal performance will require. Higher performance leads to higher expectations.

"If my performance stays where it is," their reasoning goes, "then I won't run the risk of disappointing myself or others."

The bad news is that they won't make themselves or others very happy either. This timid, failure-avoidance approach leads to repetition in personal and professional behavior. Repeating yesterday is a time-honored technique for getting from the cradle to the grave without experiencing anything really bad, or *really good.* In today's fast-paced business world, there's no future in that kind of thinking.

Repeating yesterday

Repeating yesterday can be a self-hypnotic behavior. Most people do it so regularly and effortlessly that they don't give it a thought. When I ask people if they regularly repeat yesterday, they usually reply, "Gee, I never thought about it." As soon as they think about it for a moment, they invariably admit that they habitually follow the same routines and patterns day-in and day-out.

The trance-like tendency to repeat yesterday produces a comforting feeling of *the familiar.* That's why people look at you funny when you suggest doing something a bit unorthodox or somehow differently than it's been done before. It never ceases to amaze me that the rationale given most frequently for why something is done in a particular way is "Because that's how we've always done it." You'd think that people would be ashamed to admit that such a reason is the best they can offer. Just the same, that's the answer I hear time and time again.

If a person doesn't think s/he is repeating yesterday, then s/he probably is. The 19th-century author and great thinker, Elbert Hubbard, said that stagnation is evident when the past seems bigger and more important than the future. In other words, if you're consciously attempting to approach each day in a fresh, new, innovative way, then you're certainly not repeating yesterday. Focusing on the future is a guaranteed method of breaking the cycle of stagnation and the habitual ritual of repeating yesterday.

Substance abuse

Because repeating yesterday is a way to stay in comfortable, familiar territory, and venturing into the reservoir of undeveloped strengths guarantees that things are going to change in life, it becomes easier to understand why we all have a natural inclination to remain in nonthreatening patterns. It makes as much sense as peeling a banana, eating the peel and throwing the banana away. If personal undeveloped strengths can be considered part of our essential substance, then repeating yesterday must be considered substance abuse.

People who repeat yesterday are in motion but not in *direction*. A strong sense that you're pedaling hard but going nowhere is a prime indication of cyclical repetition in your life. If you don't know where you're headed, but feel you are making good time, you've been on the treadmill too long. Effort needs to be associated with progress or hypnosis begins. Ask yourself throughout the day:

Am I in direction right now or just in motion?

Doing what doesn't work

A frighteningly common way that we repeat yesterday is by continuing to do what we already know doesn't work. It's fascinating to interrupt people who are about to do something for the umpteenth time and ask them, point blank, if they think their task is going to produce positive results. They usually give you that same funny look as before and shake their heads, "no." Once again, they are repeating behavior that they consciously know isn't getting them anywhere but do it anyway as a means of preserving the status quo.

Problems anyone?

During my tenure as a district sales manager for a large corporation, I counseled many team members about problems they encountered. One man had been selected as one of our top 10 rookies. It's not unusual for some people to get a fast start out of the blocks. However, the following year, the same man's production was near zero and not that unusual either.

When the two of us discussed his rapid decline, it became obvious that his job wasn't fun anymore. His fire had gone out. Under close examination, we discovered that, somewhere along the line, he had begun to see his customer transactions as problems. As a result, he developed the habit of carrying out 90 percent of his responsibilities by rote and stopping short of the critical 10 percent necessary to finish the job.

By unconsciously sabotaging the successful completion of his tasks, he was *avoiding* problems. In reality, he was creating bigger problems. When I asked him if he realistically expected to execute his job without encountering problems, he admitted that he could not. Moreover, when he consciously prepared himself for the problems he knew were sure to come, he wasn't afraid of them at all.

He realized that his desire had been stifled by a natural, but counterproductive, defense mechanism against encountering the unexpected. Once he committed to stoking the furnace of desire again, problems became little more than part of the landscape and he went on to exceed even his previous performance.

Low performers don't tend to leave organizations as often as high performers. One of the myths business executives tend to believe is that high performers are content and confident. The fact is that more high performers hop from organization to organization than low performers. That's why business executives sometimes look around their organization and scratch their heads when they only see mediocre performers. Low performers tend to accumulate. High performers move on. Why?

High performers, feeling pressured to maintain their level of productivity, often move to new organizations so they can use the move as an excuse for not maintaining the same high performance two years in a row.

The *personal high-performance process* allows an individual to be credited for developing personal potential over time and diminishes unreasonable expectations. Managers who understand the *personal high-performance process* will keep their high performers and simultaneously raise the performance levels of everyone else in the organization.

When problems are dragged out and exposed to the light of day, they become less intimidating. Once you are liberated from fear of encountering problems, personal performance will start to climb.

Procrastination

Gathering information or learning something new tends to wake us from repetitious slumber. Those who would rather snooze become information *deflectors* rather than information gatherers. In much the same way, when we constantly promise that we'll get to something but never seem to, we're helping to preserve the past by postponing the present.

"As long as change is in the future," their subconscious minds conclude, "nothing's going to catch me unprepared today."

People who claim that they'll get down to business *someday* are forgetting that "someday" includes "today" as much as it includes any other day. The old saying that goes, "Someday never comes" really means that people who use *someday* as their deadline are really using *never* as their schedule for action. To high-performance people, *someday* means "some now."

At least people who pledge to act in the future are bringing a tacit indictment upon themselves for being aware that, at the very least, something needs to be done that's not being done now. The greatest tragedy in repeating yesterday is that, by not looking enthusiastically toward the future, we admit that the high point of our lives is in the past, not in the future. That's not a very hopeful thought.

The new road

The only way to guarantee that tomorrow can be more exciting than yesterday is to embark on an action plan to set, pursue, and achieve new goals. No new goals means that old ones are being re-cycled. If getting up in the morning is difficult and there is little or no enthusiasm for the day ahead, there's no doubt that it's the old road that lies ahead, not a new one.

Repeating yesterday causes what former Disney executive Mike Vance, calls "psychosclerosis" or "hardening of the mind." Repeating yesterday can also be characterized as freezing at a single rung on life's ladder. It doesn't mean that no climbing has ever been done. It means that progress has stopped.

When past accomplishments occupy more daydreams than future visions, chances are good that every day starts back in the same old spot. No one in history was ever honored for how well they repeated yesterday. As a rule, honors are preserved for those who break new ground.

"Life is a lively process of becoming. If you haven't added to your interests during the past year; if you are thinking the same thoughts, relating the same personal experiences, having the same predictable reactions—rigor mortis of the personality has set in."

—General Douglas MacArthur

Exercise your potential

It only takes a couple of questions to determine where you stand in terms of current performance vs. potential performance. The exercise to determine the presence of untapped potential goes like this:

1. What am I currently earning? (Other types of accomplishment or milestones can be substituted for earnings.)
2. Do I know what I would have to do to earn more?
3. What could I earn if I had more training or knowledge?

There once was a man who hung by his fingertips from the window ledge all night long only to discover at first light that his feet were only a few inches off the ground. I've never known anyone who completed this exercise without realizing how close s/he was to significant increases in performance and the rewards that go with it. It's a real eye opener, and a little embarrassing to acknowledge that the answers to improving performance have always been so close at hand.

The mentor's eye

The best view of ourselves is usually through someone else's objective eyes. That's why mentors are invaluable. Not only do people who we respect and who respect us offer nuggets of knowledge and wisdom, they can also provide priceless powers of observation. Peers with varied agenda and loyalties are hardly a reliable source of feedback. Not that the reactions of others aren't important, all input goes in to the mix of self-assessment. However, mentors have a genuine desire to see their charges grow and develop, and they don't spare the rod or sugar-coat the truth in their effort to help.

Let me be your mentor for a moment and I'll give you some high-performance characteristics that need to be developed in healthy doses if you intend to increase personal performance and keep it high. Studying people is something I do constantly and I recommend that you make it a habit, too. My personal library at home is filled with thousands of volumes that chronicle the achievements of great men and women through the centuries. My wife and I invest every moment we can on whatever continent is necessary to spend time with people of accomplishment. I just can't get enough of these people's thoughts and actions.

Learn, do, develop

Mentors don't have to know you. They don't even have to be alive. Studying and learning from the writings of great people are activities that we can do on our own time and at our own speed. Books are chunks of people's lives that anyone can experience. There are so many men and women who have blazed trails before us that we have no excuse for thinking we're encountering problems and challenges no one has ever seen before. We can take the time to figure out what others have *already* figured out or visit the public library and tap into the experiences of those who have gone before.

There are three actions that must accompany the seven-step high-performance process if there's to be a lasting commitment to becoming a high-performance person:

1. *Learn* and *visualize* how high-performance people, past and present, *think* and *act.* This is where the diligent study of successful people comes in.

2. *Do* what high-performance people *do.*

3. *Develop* the personal characteristics of high-performance people.

1. Learn

It's important to learn and visualize how high-performance people think and act because nobody has a crystal ball with which to predict the future. If the psychics we see on television or read about in the newspaper could *really* access the future, they would rule the world instead of doing psychic readings or writing syndicated columns for a living.

Pretend for a moment that you *can* reach out five years into the future and pull back a copy of the yellow pages, your company newspaper, *The Wall Street Journal,* your tax return, or some other record of who's who and what's what. If you knew five years ago what you know now, chances are good that you'd be far better off than you are. But we can't predict the future. Neither could the successful people throughout history.

One of the first things you learn in studying the lives of high-performance people is that they didn't plan every step on their road to success. However, each and every one of them had a strong sense of who they were and what their mission in life was. High-performance people think in high-performance terms and act accordingly. They can't predict what they will encounter along life's road, but they respond to their circumstances in ways that produce positive results.

Around the turn of the last century, Orison Swett Marden said:

"Make every occasion a great occasion for you cannot tell when fate is testing you for something greater."

Looking back five years into your past, how different would your life be now, both personally and professionally, if you had thought and acted in high-performance terms when you encountered the challenges and opportunities that came your way? I've got a news flash for you. Today and every day for the rest of your life there will be challenges and opportunities that can benefit you and those around you in a more meaningful and positive way *if you resolve to think and act like a high-performance person.*

2. Do

It's possible to have all the knowledge in the world and still repeat yesterday. Learning and visualizing what high-performance people think and do will not have any effect on your future until you begin to *do* what high-performance people *do.* Even if you begin in a limited, nonthreatening way, it's critical that you begin to *act.* If you learn something and don't act on it within 72 hours, all of the time, money and energy in learning it is wasted.

Throughout my many travels and extensive interaction with business people, I find that there is a tremendous gap that exists between how people do their jobs and *how they know how to do their jobs.* There isn't a person alive who isn't aware of how s/he could do what s/he does even better. The earlier three-question exercise on current performance vs. potential performance proves that you're among those who are a hair's breadth away from breaking through in one or more areas in your life. In our effort to maintain the comfortable *familiar* we don't even do the things we already know would elevate us to the next performance level. Everyone commits self-sabotage in some way.

I've never met a person who couldn't come up with at least one idea or technique that would improve performance. Without engaging in the study and observation of high-performance people, past and present, every one of us already knows how to improve our personal performance. Therefore, think of how much farther and faster you would go if you spent some time learning and then *applying* what you've learned through *action.*

I used to think that the Nike shoes slogan, "Just Do It," was a bit naive because it didn't explain exactly what it was that we were supposed to "just do." I remembered that we all know at least *one thing* that would boost our personal performance if we "just did it." Don't be intimidated by thinking that you have to mimic every behavior of every high-performance person you ever knew or studied. Start with one behavior and go from there.

My all-time pet peeve is someone explaining someone else's success by saying that s/he was/is a "natural-born high achiever." Not true. I've written in the past about the myth of the natural-born leader and the same is true of high-performance people. There is no such thing as a "natural-born" high-performance person. High-performance people make a specific decision to stop repeating yesterday and, in doing so, are fully aware of the conscious decision to elevate personal performance.

The decision to become a high-performance person is like getting a new birthday. In truth, our high-performance birthdays should be honored more than our chronological ones. Your actual date of birth has little or nothing to do with the decisions you make later that shape and determine your life.

It's true that childhood experiences, role models, social pressures, and other factors will alter your appetite for work and accomplishment. However, a commitment to learn the things that must be learned and do the things that must be done to increase personal performance is a highly individual and completely informed decision. It doesn't happen unconsciously or by some kind of osmosis. No one is *born* with a personal commitment to high performance.

3. Develop

Learning and launching into action what we've discussed leads to the internalization of the ideas and principles involved. Learning and applying are conscious and willful acts. Over time, the more we learn and the more action we take leads to the unconscious adoption of ideas and principles as our own. When I talk about developing the personal characteristics of high-performance people, I'm talking about the natural internalization of what we consciously commit ourselves to doing in the *learn* and *do* stages.

The experience of truly becoming a high-performance person includes the literal adoption of personal and professional principles that inform the way we think and act. The cycle is complete when the thoughts and actions of high-performance people become *our own* thoughts and actions.

Remembering that what's true in your personal life is true in your professional life, it's time to build consistency into your guiding principles. If you have constant conflict between the ethical construct or lifestyle requirements of your professional position and who you choose to be in your private moments, a career change might be in order. These personality traits are present in high performers that I've observed and studied over two decades and are the key ingredients of any high-performance personality. Think what high performers think and you'll find yourself doing what high-performance people do. Do what high performers do and you'll find yourself thinking the way high performers think.

My good friend, Jim Rohn, advises poor people to take rich people out to lunch and *listen*. Most poor people would reason that the person with all the money should buy *them* lunch. According to Jim, the poor person fails to understand that most rich people were poor at one time or another and have nothing to learn from someone who hasn't been able to overcome his or her poverty. It's the poor folks whose lives can be changed by learning from more successful people and adopting their thoughts and behavior.

Critical characteristics

I've observed that the people I respect most each have an *uncompromising integrity*. Don't ask them to bend the rules, leave work early or pad their paycheck with a little creative accounting. These people understand the reasons behind rules and regulations. They're not dedicated to strict codes of conduct for the sake of militaristic uniformity. They are interested in the long-term impact of their behavior and appreciate how their consistency in the present will benefit them and their organization down the road. Uncompromising integrity makes no sense unless you're looking at the larger, long-range picture.

High-performance people are *high-energy people* who refuse to get bogged down in unimportant matters. Knowing the difference between important and interesting can shape up your day considerably. The tendency for those who repeat yesterday to distract high-performance people is epidemic. As one of my mentors once told me:

Don't walk away from negative people...run!

People who worry about the size of their paycheck more than the significance of their accomplishments instinctively try to turn the high-performance person's eyes away from important goals and entangle them in pettiness and counterproductive concerns. No one who is focused on the long-term best interests of the organization and the individuals within the organization will have time to waste on negativity and generally selfish matters.

There are big games and there are little games. High-performance people play big games. One way to gauge whether you're on the road to higher personal performance is to take note of whether you're dealing with bigger issues or smaller issues than you were a year ago, a month ago, or even a week ago.

One of the test pilots in the motion picture, *The Right Stuff*, had a terrific line. He said, "You never know how far you can go until you've gone too far." Are you holding yourself back because you're afraid of going too far? The truth is, nature has ways of telling us when we're going too far and we can adjust accordingly. There are natural barriers that define real limits. Our self-imposed barriers will never allow us to know the full range of our possibilities—unless we push our self-imposed barriers back. We never know the real meaning of the word "yes" until we encounter the word "no." It's the word "stop" that gives meaning to the word "go."

High-performance people are *tough-minded problem-solvers* who are stable under pressure. They're confidence is boosted by their commitment to keeping their lives moving forward. High-performance people know how to *work priorities*. Simply making lists and assigning priorities isn't enough. Anybody can do that. In fact, most people who make priority lists turn right around and ignore them.

Every one of us has made a priority list, ranking tasks from most important to least important and then jumped into the list somewhere in the middle. *Working priorities* means the top item on the list gets full energy until it's finished. As soon as that task is accomplished, the next item moves to the top of the list and gets the same treatment until every item gets its turn as the number-one item on the list. High-performance people never treat minor tasks as unimportant because they started at the bottom of a list. At some point in time, every item has its turn at the top of the list.

High-performance people are *courageous*. Safe plodders seldom end up at the head of the pack. High-performance people are not afraid to put the other foot down. Someone who leaves one foot dangling is waiting for everything to be right before s/he proceeds. Another news flash: If everything is right, if all conditions are perfect (which they never are), it would only be for a moment. By the time your foot hit the pavement, something, somewhere along the line, would have changed.

In other words, waiting for everything to be right before proceeding means that you'll never get started, which is exactly *why* the repeating yesterday crowd does it. None of the famous inventors, explorers, leaders, scientists, change agents of any kind would be household names if they hadn't had the courage to take risks. If fear calls the shots in your life, your life will be spent in hiding. High-performance people make a point to do the things that they fear.

Have you ever done something that you feared, and survived to tell about it? If you have, I don't have to describe the feeling of exhilaration that goes along with it. Why not get that feeling on a regular basis? It's like waking up your taste buds with a wonderful delicacy. It never ceases to feel great. The more the circle of self-imposed barriers is pushed back, the more your sense of pleasure and reward comes back to life.

I've seen employees literally resurrected from emotional death by intentionally stepping out of their comfort zone. Good things can still happen to you when fear is in charge of your life. Taking the initiative to *make things happen* is evidence that you've taken command over your fear. Fear and confidence are mutually exclusive. Either you or your fear is in charge of your personal and professional lives.

High-performance people are *committed* and *dedicated hard workers*. These people are the first in the office and the last to leave. They love what they do and can't get enough of it. Don't confuse workaholism, which serves to avoid personal responsibilities, with genuine enthusiasm. People don't die from hard work in a job they love. However, workaholism can kill. I believe that work is a basic human need and we can't be fulfilled unless we are committed to some type of task.

High-performance people are *unorthodox* and have an *urge to create.* Leaders who want to have a record-breaking, pace-setting organization will choose an unorthodox and creative person over the safe, compliant bureaucrat every time. I've had people work for me that absolutely drove me up a wall. I'm not talking about loose cannons, but rather dedicated people who aren't afraid to try the unusual without permission and ask forgiveness later.

Many managers act as if unorthodox people are somehow threatening their precious authority. Forget it. Any leader worth his or her salt knows that his or her own success will be enhanced by the enthusiastic creativity and drive of unorthodox and creative people. It might take some getting used to at first, but the payoff is tremendous.

To increase your personal performance by acting more unorthodox and creative, you must help out those around you by being understanding and sensitive to the fact that your change will take some getting used to by others. It's unreasonable to expect everyone you live with or work with to immediately accept you new image. When they do though, you'll be happier and they'll be more excited and entertained by the relationship.

Perfect failures are more palatable than *screw-ups* and less likely to impede future efforts. Learning from failed efforts means that the effort was not a total failure. What we customarily consider to be wasted effort isn't wasted at all if it provides us with knowledge of what not to do and, therefore, helps streamline the future.

High-performance people have the *goal orientation* to face tough decisions. Being able to focus on the goal is essential to keeping all energies flowing toward it. As always, the high-performance person will be tempted by distractions from those who find it easier and more comfortable to avoid goals. Many people willfully avoid setting goals and focusing their energies because they want to avoid accepting responsibility for the outcome, good or bad, at all costs. If the going is tough, staying focused on the goal will always bring the exercise to a faster conclusion and diminish the discomfort you may experience along the way.

On the surface, refusing to accept responsibility for how good we can become doesn't make much sense. Dig a little deeper and it becomes apparent that these people are not avoiding how good they can become as much as they're avoiding the perceived obligation to keep getting better once they begin to improve. They know that staying in a rut is a way to maintain control in life despite the knowledge that a better life is outside of the rut. At least the rut is certain, familiar, and predictable.

Goals need to precede self-discipline, not the other way around. Many people use the excuse that they're not ready for goals because they lack structure in their lives. Goals and the need to focus on something beyond yourself are invaluable to creating and maintaining structure and order. You're not going to arrive at your destination safely if you drive with your eyes fixed on the rear-view mirror. You might as well not have a destination at all.

High-performance people have *inspired enthusiasm*. This isn't the first time I've mentioned enthusiasm. Yet it's important enough to have its own mention. Enthusiasm, whether it's present or absent, is contagious. People around you get what you've got. That's what determines whether people want to be around you or want to avoid you.

Fall back on your own experience to confirm this one. Who do you want to be around and who do you prefer to avoid? You might not enjoy being in the presence of a screaming maniac who is spewing so much enthusiasm that you come away with stains on your clothes, but genuinely enthusiastic people are fun to be around. Genuinely lethargic or downright negative people are not much fun to be around. The choice is yours.

High-performance people are *realistic* and can organize turbulent situations. All of the enthusiasm and energy I've been describing doesn't mean that high-performance people have their heads in the clouds. These people are not likely to sit around and cry over spilled milk. Neither do they cling to the sordid details of a recent episode in their lives and bore you to tears as they recite them.

To the high-performance person, all of the characteristics I've listed are grounded in *reality*. It would be nice if people, left to their own devices, were always kind and generous with one another or sought to build one another up at every opportunity. Unfortunately, only a few people are like that. It would also be nice if money and creature comforts didn't take precedence over the needs of others in most people's lives. Wouldn't it be great if all people wanted desperately to work and grow in their personal and professional lives, and were willing to invest themselves in a career, starting at the bottom?

The list could go on and on. The point is that, although many things *would be nice*, they simply aren't realistic. High-performance people always strive toward benefiting the most people, most of the time. However, they're realistic enough to acknowledge the difference between the exception and the rule. In doing so, high-performance people are far better equipped to achieve meaningful accomplishments and not waste their time on Pollyanna pursuits that ultimately benefit no one.

High-performance people know that mistakes happen. They're aware that people frequently fail to do what they say they'll do. They understand that circumstances change and that life is not always fair. Nonetheless, they accept those things that can't be changed and move forward in spite of them. Life may not be perfect, but human beings, guided by immutable principles, have a tremendous capacity to adapt in an ever-changing environment.

Finally, high-performance people have a desire to help others grow. I don't think it's possible for someone to truly be committed to the high-performance process without helping others do the same thing. Except in the rarest of circumstances, we don't live and work in isolation. There is always someone, at some level, to interact with.

Synergy can only occur when there are multiple parties to contend with. Anyone with management experience knows that a group of people can have a collective negative energy or a collective positive energy. The negative energy is produced by self-absorption, invariably modeled by leadership. Positive energy is produced by team members making a concerted effort to help those around them—internal and external customers. Like the negative environment, the *positive* energy must be modeled and encouraged by the people in the visible leadership roles.

When people are wandering aimlessly and don't know what to focus on, my first advice is to find someone to help. In the absence of any other specific directive, helping someone else grow and succeed is, in and of itself, an effective and life-changing goal that will produce structure and direction to end the drifting.

It makes a difference

Striving to improve personal performance is like running a race with no finish line. The process never ends as long as the high-performance person is alive. Bob Hope, Dr. Norman Vincent Peale, Mother Teresa, Norman Rockwell, and Grandma Moses are only a few examples of people who have demonstrated no desire to ever stop getting better at what they do. Every one of them has or had a never-ending dedication to the principles I've just described.

The high-performance person won't accept 99.9 percent as "good enough." Natalie Gabal listed a series of effects that accepting 99.9 percent would have on our lives:

1. Two million documents would be lost this year by the IRS.
2. 811,000 faulty rolls of 35mm film would be loaded into cameras this year.
3. 22,000 checks would be deducted from the wrong bank account in the next 60 minutes.
4. 12 babies would be given to the wrong parents each day.
5. 268,500 defective tires would be shipped this year.
6. 2,488,200 books would be shipped this year with the wrong covers.
7. Two airliner landings each day at O'Hare Airport would be unsafe.

8. 3,056 copies of tomorrow's edition of *The Wall Street Journal* would be missing three sections.
9. 18,322 pieces of mail would be mishandled in the next hour.
10. 291 pacemaker operations will be performed incorrectly this year.

A way of life

Dedicating yourself to the *high-performance process* means committing your talents and energies to an ongoing agenda. It's not something you do from nine to five and then leave at the office. Becoming a high-performance person is more than a way of working, it's a way of living.

To summarize this overview, I can't improve on the words of Phillips Brooks, so I'll just pass them on:

Once you discover that you've only been living half a life, the other half will haunt you until you develop it.

Your Moment of Truth:
Selecting the Desired Rewards

"The bravest are surely those who have the clearest vision of what is before them, glory and danger alike, and yet notwithstanding, go out to meet it."

—Thucydides

The quality of our lives is a direct result of the choices we make. That makes how we go about making choices very important. Having those *different kinds of eyes* I mentioned earlier becomes increasingly valuable as we attempt to peer into the future. We can't, of course. Peer into the future, that is. We can only *predict* what we *think* the future might bring, based upon our present knowledge and experience.

Stunt man/filmmaker Hal Needham decided to jump a California riverbed with a rocket-powered pickup truck. This kind of stunt was not unusual for Hal. However, it was one of his more dangerous endeavors. I asked him if he was ever bothered by his mortality. I wondered if he ever considered that this kind of behavior could cost him his life.

When I confronted him with the fact that he was playing a high-stakes, life-and-death game, he calmly replied, "If I'm killed doing one of these stunts, I'll have the comfort of knowing that I died doing exactly what I wanted to be doing." Hal is still alive. He's been mighty banged-up over the years, but he's still around, doing exactly what he loves to do.

Weighing the pros and cons of your actions in terms of future consequences is a constant challenge. If your eyes are fixed on what lies ahead of you, then you're at least pointed in the right direction. One of the reasons so many people fixate on the past and literally *back* into the future is to avoid facing the dreaded *moment of truth*.

In our moment of truth or turning point, each of us must call upon our life experiences and accumulated knowledge, as well as our best instincts, to make decisions. What scares most folks is that they must also bear responsibility for the wisdom or folly of their decisions. In not turning around and looking squarely into the potential positive *and* negative consequences of their decisions, some people feel as if they can avoid responsibility for the outcome.

Unfortunately, for them, there's no way to avoid responsibility, regardless of the outcome. The axiom, *Not to decide is to decide*, is so common it's almost a cliché. Nevertheless, for many people, it's somehow emotionally less threatening to passively allow the future to take its course without making any effort to set the stage for it.

Going through life without facing moments of truth is like piloting a rudderless ship. If ending up wherever the wind and current take you is preferable to accepting responsibility for plotting your own course, you're not ready for the *high-performance process*. High-performance people have definite intentions about life and how they want to live it. They weren't necessarily born that way, but somewhere along the line they decided to take charge of their lives.

The courage of a 5-year-old

Children often cut to the chase much more fearlessly than adults do. Observing children reveals much about human character that adults have become too adept at hiding. Predicting the potential cost of our decisions is relative to what we value most. Our decision-making courage or cowardice is measured by the potential downside consequences of our decisions. When I observe someone add up the positives and negatives, contemplate the consequences, and then boldly make a decision, I'm impressed. I'm impressed by people who aren't afraid to ask the *hard questions*.

My grandson Rex was in kindergarten when he caught a case of spring fever. It hadn't been too long ago in his young life that he had the freedom to come and go with his mother as their schedules allowed. So he probably thought he had a good chance of convincing his mom to play hooky with him for a day.

Living in Southern California, Rex was well aware of the many diversions that would make excellent alternatives to a day in the classroom.

"Mom, it's too beautiful today to go to school. Can we go to the beach?" he asked.

"No, honey," his mom replied. "You have to go to school today."

Rex figured that the destination he had suggested wasn't enticing enough to gain his mother's compliance.

"Then how about Disneyland? Think of the fun we could have there," the little salesman continued.

"No, Rex," his mother countered, hip to his trick, "you have to go to school today."

Rex was en route to a moment of truth, his own turning point you might say

"Why?" Rex was taking the argument to a new level.

Facing her own moment of truth, she decided to appeal to her son's sympathies.

"Because if you don't go to school, they could put me in jail."

He looked at her for about two seconds, put his hands on his hips, cocked his head to one side and asked,

"For how long?"

My daughter was correct in thinking that she had steered her son to his own moment of truth. However, she didn't realize that he hadn't *quite* arrived. As far as he was concerned, all options weren't exhausted yet. In short, the potential negative consequences of *his* decision grew out of a different set of priorities. She had hoped to make the decision for him by placing him in an untenable position. But, as she turned more cards over on the table, he simply asked to see the next card.

None of us can claim to have truly experienced a moment of truth until we have looked at all the cards. Only looking at the good cards or the bad cards means we aren't fully accepting the challenge to make the best-informed decision possible.

Selecting desired rewards

To this point, I've attempted to heighten your awareness of how much your personal success depends upon your total commitment. As we stand at our personal turning point, each of us determines where it is we want to go and what we want when we get there. Recognizing that nothing worth having comes easy and the good always comes with some measure of the bad, we set a course and lay out our flight plan accordingly.

We have much more control over our destinations, or rewards if you prefer, than we do the route to achieving them. Once in a while we might get lucky and negotiate our plotted course flawlessly. It's more likely, however, that we'll need to alter our course many times along the way to accommodate uncharted obstacles and other variables beyond our control.

What keeps us returning to the stated goal is whatever we feel makes the new effort worthwhile. Like my grandson Rex demonstrated, it's not the reward we seek that drives us forward as much as how badly we desire it. We might have to alter course many times or even plot one or more *new* courses in the pursuit of our desired rewards. A high-performance person might also put it this way: *Many roads lead to the goal.* You must be looking forward to keep your eyes on the prize.

Butt snappers

As jet fighters were being introduced to the Air Force, a problem arose with ejection seats. Jets flew faster and higher than their propeller predecessors and pilot ejection, in cases of emergency, became a more sophisticated and dangerous predicament. Ejection seats were separated from the cockpit by an explosive charge equal to a 35mm artillery shell to insure that the pilot cleared the aircraft before the parachute deployed.

The pilot simply needed to roll forward out of the seat once clear of the aircraft and the parachute would be free to open. Unfortunately, a common problem started to pop up (no pun intended) in some ejections. Some pilots would pull up both arm rests exposing the ejection seat triggers and squeeze them detonating the explosive that launched the pilot and seat 150 to 175 feet above the aircraft.

Then, instead of letting go, some pilots kept a death grip on the seat handles, reluctant to separate themselves from the last tangible piece of the airplane that had, until then, always been a safe place. As long as the pilot remained in the ejection seat, the parachute remained trapped against the seat back, unable to open. Striking the ground at 200 miles-per-hour, still sitting in an ejection seat with an unopened parachute *will* ruin your whole day!

The Air Force went back to the ejection seat manufacturers with the problem and the government contractors returned with a solution. The new design called for a 2-inch webbed strap that attached to the front edge of the seat, under the pilot and behind him, and attached to an electronic take-up reel behind the headrest. Two seconds after ejection, the electronic take-up reel would immediately take up the slack, forcing the pilot forward out of the seat thus freeing the parachute to open. The pilot was "butt-snapped" to safety.

A body in motion tends to remain in motion and a body at rest tends to remain at rest until acted upon by an external force. Dr. Alexis Carrel used this definition of inertia in a sentence:

Life leaps like a geyser for those who drill through the rock of inertia.

In a seminar, I once quoted Dr. Carrel and gave a lengthy dissertation on the role of external forces to overcoming inertia. After I had finished, one of those in attendance came up to me and winked.

"I know what you're trying to say about overcoming inertia," the man said. "What you mean to say is that we need butt snappers on every chair around the office."

A butt-snapper, as he described it, is something akin to a spring-loaded *whoopee cushion.* The bottom line is that, when detonated, it launches your rear end out of the chair. So, if words like *external forces overcoming inertia* leave you uninspired, think about what *butt snappers* on everyone's chairs would do to productivity around the office. Think about how much a *butt snapper* on your own chair would do for your personal productivity.

The tough road

A man I'm proud to call my friend had a troubled childhood. So troubled, in fact, that he graduated from not one, but *two* reform schools. Later in his life he went on to make two multimillion-dollar fortunes in separate fields. He told me once that he made the second fortune just to prove to himself that the first one wasn't luck. I like his spirit.

When I asked him how he did it, he told me that he asked himself four questions. But unlike most people, he *listened* to his answers. Until he pointed it out, I hadn't realized how often we ask ourselves probing questions without listening to the answers. The answers are always there when we engage in self-inventory. Unfortunately, we simply ignore them most of the time or note only the portions that don't present a major personal threat. The questions always seem harmless enough; it's the *answers* that are scary.

It's time to turn off the easy road to nowhere and take the harder road to where you can genuinely feel happy and satisfied. Truthful answers to tough questions become landmarks along your journey. If you question your own candor, just imagine that you've been shot with sodium pentothal (truth serum) and have no choice but to answer truthfully.

Question 1: What do I really want?

There has to be some reason for all the hard work you do. We never do anything for *no reason.* If it seems that way at times, it's because we're in such an ingrained pattern that we're functioning in a trance. How many times has someone startled you awake by asking, "What are you doing?" Whatever it was that you were doing, you were doing it in a trance.

Why were you doing something so familiar and redundant that you were in a trance? Why had that activity become such a habit that you could do it while semiconscious? Ultimately there was a reason. And so it is with everything we do. Whether we do it in a trance or with hyper-focus, there is a conscious or an unconscious reason for everything we do.

If someday you look back down your life's course and say, "That's what I proudly did with my life," what landmarks would you be looking at? A friend and mentor of mine once asked me, "Wouldn't it be Hell if someday God showed you what you *could* have done with your life?" Since then I've often wondered if I would want to sit down some day, after I've graduated to the other side and watch *"The Life And Times Of Danny Cox—As They Should Have Been."* Would you want to watch your movie?

You propel yourself closer to your selected rewards when you make conscious choices to do what you do for *good* reasons. If the reason behind every action is well thought out, then each action works in concert with every other action to keep things moving toward your desired rewards. Identifying what you want and making sure that everything you do moves you closer to that goal takes much of the chance out of your personal success equation.

Question 2: What does it cost?

Talk about mitigating factors. If defining desired rewards is important to motivation, then evaluating potential costs is important to avoiding *demotivation.* As my grandson Rex figured out, there is a line that needs to be drawn that establishes when the desired reward is no longer desirable because the cost is too high.

Cost evaluation is often improperly used as an excuse for not boldly trying something new. While it's irresponsible to set goals without considering the negative implications, it's just as irresponsible to misrepresent the potential liabilities of positive action. As with so many things in life, it's appropriate to strike a healthy balance between courage and caution.

A bang-up lesson

Teaching people about costs is a powerful behavior modification tool, just like rewards are. While getting rewards for appropriate behavior is always more pleasant than receiving some form of punishment, the two influences have been known to shape what we do. I had a radar observer I'll call *Gibs (fighter-pilot lingo for "guy in back seat")* who flew in the rear seat of my F-101 fighter during my Air Force days. Gibs was a good example of how costs can influence behavior.

Gibs and I were on alert status during a war games exercise at an Air Force base outside of Tucson, Arizona. Alert status means that you've got to be ready to go at the sound of an alarm. It doesn't matter if you're sound asleep. When the alarm rings, the pilot and radar observer have to go from a sound sleep to being airborne in under five minutes. Stopping to shower, shave and read the newspaper was out.

Obviously there is a great amount of training, preparation and coordination between flight crew and ground crew involved. Gibs and I had rehearsed the exercise thousands of times. Everything from our flight suits to the seat belt harnesses in the cockpit were precisely preset to maximize efficiency of movement when the time came to *scramble.*

It was a regular ballet. No wasted motion could be tolerated. Every detail of the preflight and take off process had been memorized and rehearsed until it was second nature. One hand was starting engines and adjusting throttles while the other hand was buckling belts and moving on to another hundred small-but-critical tasks—all without stopping to think about them. Ultimately, the idea was to get off the ground and engage the enemy before the enemy catches you on the ground.

The Air Force brass wasn't at all happy with poor performance in the war games that measured our country's military preparedness. The positive rewards we received for superior performance were decorations and honors for our outfit. However, among the costs of poor performance was a concentrated dose of what was already grueling training.

Gibs and I were sleeping in the alert barn located near the end of the runway where the fighters were poised for immediate departure when the "scramble" horn went off. Instantly, we were in our flight suits and climbing into the cockpit. Literally within moments I was swinging the fighter onto the runway in a rolling take off. When I lit both afterburners it felt like we had been rear-ended. Within 13 seconds we went from 0 to 200 miles per hour.

The ballet seemed flawless with each movement becoming more like instinct than learned behavior. So it was not unnatural to be instantly aware of any deviation in the pattern. But deviation there was. Almost the moment we became airborne I noticed a loud banging. It was not like any sound I had heard before. It sounded like somebody was outside the aircraft using a jackhammer on the fuselage.

The canopy was closed and there was no way to confirm visually or with instruments what was causing the banging. I requested a fly-by so the crew in the control tower could examine the exterior of the aircraft. The tower reported seeing nothing unusual. About then Gibs informed me that, in the haste of our departure, he had forgotten to fasten his shoulder harness. The big metal buckles were dangling outside the canopy where they had been preset for quick attachment as he got settled into his seat. Now they were banging against the metal skin of the aircraft. At speeds of several hundred miles per hour the buckles were banging pretty hard. I immediately decided to abort the flight and land the aircraft. There was no telling how much damage those buckles could do.

Gibs sheepishly admitted that he forgot to fasten his seat belt, too. Maybe to redeem himself he offered to cut the straps loose. I instantly had a vision of the big metal buckles getting sucked into the air intake of the left engine. That would have been sure disaster. I instructed Gibs to leave the straps where they were and I landed the aircraft with the straps hanging on either side of the cockpit.

It seemed like the entire United States Air Force was waiting for us when we taxied in. As we taxied, Gibs said, "I think I'm in trouble." I replied, "I know you're in trouble." As you can imagine, we had not been a shining example of American military preparedness that day and we had brought embarrassment upon our outfit in front of the combat readiness inspection team from headquarters. Our local commanders were not pleased.

Gibs and I went through an interrogation the likes of which I had never seen before. All Gibs had done was forget to fasten his shoulder harness, yet it had nearly brought down our aircraft. After we had been grilled by our commanding officers, Gibs was sent out to pay the price for his oversight and the cost *was* high.

Carrying a 65-pound ladder and wearing his crash helmet and parachute, he had to do a complete cockpit preflight preparation in every one of the 18 fighters in our group—by himself. In the 110-degree Tucson sun, Gibs got so hot that his body stopped perspiring. It doggoned near killed the man, but the brass had a point to make and Gibs had a lesson to learn. Gibs was practically staggering when he reported back to the commander who asked him, "Do you have any questions about how to set up the cockpit of an F-101?"

About a year later, in a similar exercise near Nellis Air Force Base outside of Las Vegas, Gibs and I heard a slow thumping while in flight. Almost before I could ask Gibs if he heard the thumping, he shouted, "It's not my shoulder straps." Gibs had learned the cost of not fastening his shoulder harness and there was no other malfunction at that moment that posed as much of a threat to him as the cost of not flawlessly executing his preflight exercise. The thumping was caused this time by a mechanical malfunction that was later corrected.

Rewards are great motivators, but sometimes so are the potential costs. Never take the costs too lightly. They're always an important part of the decision-making equation.

Question 3: Am I willing to pay the price?

Before my grandson Rex was willing to answer question three, he wanted a precise assessment of the price to be paid. After his torture in the hot Arizona sun, Gibs didn't need much reminding that the price for negligence during war games was too high to consider for any reason. To Rex, the price of his mother spending some time behind bars might have been worth a day at *Disneyland,* providing the sentence wasn't too long. Of course, it wasn't a price that he had to pay *directly* either.

There will always be a price to pay for a worthwhile goal. Achieving our desired rewards, whether they are personal, social, or professional, will cost us something. Time, effort, and the opportunity to be doing something else are all things that we potentially give up when pursuing our goals.

Too high a price

Another of my less humorous Air Force experiences illustrates what can happen when the price is too high and the person faced with paying it is unwilling. I was stationed in the Philippine Islands and running intercepts on a simulated target aircraft the day I witnessed a mid-air collision between two Philippines Air Force (PAF) fighters.

There were scattered clouds that day and the Filipino pilots were also running air intercept exercises. With jet aircraft zipping in and out of the clouds at several hundred miles per hour, there's a heightened need for care and vigilance. It was also a mountainous region and, as the saying goes in the Air Force, some of the lower clouds have "rocks" in them.

I was on my way to intercept my target when I noticed the two PAF aircrafts coming dangerously close to each other. I assumed they would break away to avoid each other when I momentarily lost sight of them in a cloud. Philippine and United States military operations were separate and I had no radio contact. It became apparent that they had collided when I saw a puff of black smoke and one of the fighters spiraling out of the cloud toward the earth. The other airplane had apparently disintegrated.

As I spotted the Philippine fighter going in, the aircraft didn't appear to be unflyable. I decided to abort my intercept and dove down to catch up with the earth-bound pilot. As I caught up with him, the pilot didn't appear to be unconscious. His head was erect and he appeared to be looking forward. I rolled my aircraft in front of him to make sure he could see me. He didn't respond. I tried calling him on the emergency frequency and even used hand signals to get his attention, all to no avail.

I got an eerie feeling on top of the adrenaline rush of the crisis. I knew he could see me but he wouldn't respond. I was there to be whatever help I could be. I tried giving him more hand signals to eject or pull out of his spiral. Still no response. I was convinced he knew exactly what I was doing. He was simply seized up by panic, or "clanked" as we called it.

It was downright creepy watching another fighter pilot disappear into the clouds still at the controls of his fighter. He simply didn't want to be helped. An investigation of the wreckage a few days later revealed that he never did try to eject. As it turned out, he was the only Filipino pilot I knew personally. Neither he nor I recognized each other in those frenzied few moments as anything other than fellow pilots.

In the Air Force, a "graveyard spiral" is like being in a rut with a sudden stop at the end. My Filipino friend apparently rode his graveyard spiral all the way to the ground because he was not willing to pay what, to him, was too high a cost for the chance to survive the mid-air collision. In his mind, culture, and worldview, the price he paid with his life cost him less than the alternative of survival. Although this example is admittedly extreme, the point is well taken. In the Filipino pilot's moment of truth, he asked himself whether he was willing to pay the price. I witnessed his answer through confused and helpless eyes.

Question 4: When is the best time to start paying the price?

Now, stop and think about it. If you've decided that you're willing to pay the price to achieve your desired rewards, then what could possibly make delay worthwhile? The future is nothing more than a series of *nows* approaching you, all in a row. Sure, if you miss the present *now,* there will be another one right behind it. But what's the point of letting any of them go by without enriching them with positive, progressive action?

By the time you reach the end of this sentence, someone, somewhere, will have taken a positive, progressive action. It happens just that quickly. Because each positive, progressive action propels you closer to achieving your desired rewards, seizing the first available moment makes sense. Our parents and grandparents used to say, "Never leave until tomorrow what can be done today." British author and flamboyant personality, Quentin Crisp, said:

Don't take too long to decide.
You can become what you don't want to be.

You already know, from personal experience, how good it feels to wake up knowing that an important project or a series of smaller but equally vital, tasks are behind you and not still waiting to be done. The future becomes the past the instant that it passes the control point known as *now*. I call *now* the *control point* because neither the future nor the past can be controlled. The only place we can influence what happens to us is in the present.

Boeing Aircraft Corporation came out with some great advertisements several years ago. The advertisements featured a beautiful blue sky with the caption, "Tomorrow you can be anywhere." Below the photograph the copy continued:

"All of us have dreams of going off someday to a special someplace, to a lonely beach, to an historic city, back home."

Another ad featured a couple walking along a white, sandy beach with the surf rolling in. The copy read:

"Someday we'll take off, just the two of us. No kids, no pets, no worries. We'll lay on a lonely beach and plan another hundred years together."

Then came the challenge:

"Remember the first time you mentioned going away? How many somedays ago was that? Is your warm and wonderful someday ever really going to happen?"

The final advertisement in the three-part series featured Venice, Italy, at sunset with romantic gondolas gliding by in the foreground. The message read:

"Someday we're going to see the other side of the world. As soon as the kids are grown...or after retirement...or maybe after that."

What's after *that?* It's *now* that makes all the difference. The only place we can act is in the *now*. If the price is worth paying, it's worth paying *now*. Even though it sounds so simple, it's still hard to get moving. There is something inherently scary about making that step or taking that leap. I've already explained how accepting responsibility for our actions is often a frightening thought that freezes us up. The only place we can freeze up is *now*.

Types of goals

When setting out to identify what it is you truly *want,* it's crucial to understand what type of goal you're dealing with. There are basically three types of goals:

1. Financial Goals.
2. Lifestyle Goals.
3. Personal Growth Goals.

Financial goals are most often what people consider first. There's nothing wrong in that. Financial resources seem to represent a sort of universal language. British author and playwright Somerset Maugham, said it this way:

Money is like a sixth sense. Without it you can not fully appreciate the other five.

The lifestyle goals deal with how you want to live. It's one thing to have financial resources. It's something altogether different to decide what exactly you're going to do with your money. My grandson Rex, was contemplating how to spend his mother's money and freedom in light of a lifestyle choice.

The questions of where to live and how to live pale in comparison to the question, "What should I live for?" That's an issue of personal growth. It's possible, even commonplace, to be completely consumed with the acquisition and allocation of financial resources without ever considering *who you are* as a human being. Yet it's an unwritten law that we must grow personally if we're to continue making bigger and better things happen in our lives.

All goals, whether they be *financial, lifestyle,* or *personal growth,* must also be *realistic, measurable, challenging,* and, therefore, *exciting.* How, or why for that matter, would you want to invest the energy to break through that rock of inertia, if the goal you seek isn't exciting?

When I asked my friend who had graduated from two different reform schools how *big* my goals should be, he answered, "Big enough to turn you on." If you're feeling a little depressed, unmotivated, or uninspired, you obviously don't have any goals that *turn you on.* Each one of us has the ability to set goals that excite us. The secret to what excites each of us is found within our personal compositions. The terrific promise in your moment of truth is that what you elect to pursue can and should stimulate you.

Present problems and their relationship to goal-setting

Goal-setting and problem-solving are so similar that they are often scarcely distinguishable. Goals should be more than new outcomes somewhere in the future. Goals should also be a commitment to solve problems of the past that continue to contaminate the present. Many people tell me that they tried goal-setting in the past and it didn't work.

They say it felt like their feet were nailed to the floor and they just couldn't get anywhere no matter how much energy they exerted. When people share these experiences with me, I immediately suspect that there are unresolved past problems acting like an anchor. That's why your *first goal* must be the solution to whatever is weighing you down. Cutting your future loose from anchors of the past is essential to goal attainment.

Executive insomnia

I love all of the programs I conduct on personal high performance, leadership, and customer service. However, I get particular satisfaction out of a three-hour program I do for senior executives at large corporations. I was once a senior executive for one of the nation's largest firms and I know where the skeletons are hidden. In learning how not to rock the boat, I learned what *rocks* the boat. Moreover, I've now spent the better part of 20 years conducting seminars for and consulting with businesses large and small. My finger is on the proverbial pulse.

It's my personal mission to keep these top executives awake—not only for the three hours of the seminar, but for many nights thereafter. I want to rattle as many cages as I can. I want to stomp on their mental toes. I now live for the once-repressed freedom to speak out and tackle the difficult issues and ask the hard questions for which I would have been ostracized when I was on the corporate payroll.

You can imagine how much I enjoy being invited to address the folks at the top. Let me describe the scene. These upper-level seminars are held, of course, in the *upper room* somewhere in the *ivory tower*. Like the problems that most large companies like to keep hidden, the boardroom is a very private place known as the *sanctum sanctorum,* truly the *holy of holys.*

There is always a breathtaking conference table featuring inlaid, exotic, imported woods or marble. The executives take their appointed places around this corporate *altar* and watch the next person up the food chain for cues on when to speak and when to remain silent. I now stand in front of richly paneled walls recalling how intimidating this whole scene was back when the person at the head of the table signed my paycheck and I had to keep a sharp eye on the person up the food chain as well as the next person down the food chain.

Even though, as a consultant, the same person still pays my fee, I now get my fee up front. The head honcho expects me to come in and shape up the staff, not the president or the CEO. Wrong. I stand, knee-deep in plush carpet, no longer intimidated as I was as an employee, but bursting with excitement about the journey I'm about to launch these people on. Little do they know that the president and/or CEO will be in the bow of the boat. These conferences are fun for me because I take no prisoners. I grant these highly paid executives no quarter.

As soon as the bell sounds for round one (usually a droll introduction by a starchy CEO), I turn to the highest-ranking executive in the room and ask, "Do you have problem-solving meetings at this company?" The answer comes back as if it were recorded on a wire. "We most certainly do." The explanation usually goes something like this:

"Every week we meet in this very room and I personally conduct the problem-solving meeting. The executive vice president, the senior vice president, the first vice president, the human resources director, the training director and every other key player are present."

At this point I ask if there is anyone else present at the meetings. The president or CEO thinks for a moment and appears to be stumped. I prompt the executive a little.

"How about your secretary?"

"Of course," comes the reply. "Someone has to take notes and distribute them."

I play dumb.

"Then everyone here has the minutes from last week's problem-solving meeting?"

"Of course we do," comes the confident reply once more. "We have them in our offices, on the shelf in silk-screened three-ring binders, filed by week, month and year."

Then I make my move.

"Then what I would like everyone to do is get up right now, go back to your offices and come back with last week's problem-solving meeting notes."

They start to get up, a little annoyed that they weren't told in advance to bring the notes with them. I stop them before they get out of their chairs.

"Wait a minute, there's more" I continue. "Also bring some meeting notes from six months ago, one year ago, two years ago, and three years ago."

By now they begin sinking back into their seats. Someone nervously says, "Let's do that later. Right now let's just go on with the seminar."

"This is the seminar." I insist, knowing full well that they don't want to fetch their notes because I'm going to point out that the same problems have remained unsolved for six months, one year, 18 months or more. I'll save you, the reader, the cost of an upper-level executive seminar by simply asking, "How long have you been working on the same list of problems?"

The longer the period of time that you've been working on the same set of problems, the more comfortable your set of problems must be. People laugh nervously when I say that in my seminars. It's a disturbing notion to many to think that problems can be "comfortable." But they are and that's why we tend to keep them around like a favorite old sweater.

If I could just snap my fingers and solve the problems that have been holding you back, most people would panic and begin to hyperventilate. They would feel naked.

"What would I do at work tomorrow?" They would ask.

"How about make progress?" I would calmly respond. "What had you planned to work on tomorrow?"

Most people don't realize that they purposefully keep their desk piled high with problems so that they have something to worry and stew about from morning till night. Is that you? Do you have a Ph.D. in worrying and stewing? Your assignment is to identify which problems should be at the top of your goals list.

Top the list

The sodium pentothal is still flowing through your veins; you cannot avoid the truth. You must answer honestly. The first question to ask in identifying the problem(s) that are holding you back:

What is my biggest unresolved problem?

Answer carefully. The problem that pops into your head may not be the correct answer. Remember that we play all sorts of conscious and unconscious mental tricks on ourselves in order to maintain a comfortable and familiar security zone around us. What your mind offers up as a major problem might be a diversion. The one true test that reveals what your biggest unresolved problem really is comes in the answer to this question:

What do I spend most of my day dealing with?

Behavior speaks louder than words. What we say and what we do are often two different things. Our stated intentions might be very admirable. However, it's what we actually *do* that reveals our real priorities. If you log a week of your life, it will become apparent where your priorities are.

I don't mean look at your calendar alone and note what you intend to do. Calendar entries account for very little of the actual time we spend on this planet. Logging your day means actually stopping periodically and spending a few minutes noting what you've been spending your time doing. Many people avoid the task of logging their day because they truly don't want to know what they spend their time doing.

It might sound like I'm accusing every human being of avoiding the truth. The truth is, I think we *all* tend to focus on what preserves the familiar status quo and avoid making ourselves aware of the things that present personal challenges. It's a conscious and willful choice to become a high-performance person. Becoming a high-performance person and expanding the horizons of personal achievement is an unnatural decision that leads to extraordinary achievement.

If you feel like all of this questioning and personal reflection is leading you to the very extremes of your comfort zone, then it's *working.* Stay with it. Change is seldom comfortable, especially if it's taking you into unfamiliar territory. However, it is always exciting. Like my reform school-graduate friend says, if it's not stimulating and exciting, what's the point?

So find out what you do all day long and therein will be the real answer to the question, *What's my biggest unresolved problem?*

Now that you're aware that your biggest unresolved problem is probably serving to keep you going around in circles, you simply need to spot the circles. Find the biggest circle and you've found the biggest problem.

Once you've identified what your biggest unresolved problem is and you have it at the top of your goals list, the next question becomes:

What am I doing about it?

This question has pretty much been answered already. Nevertheless, it's important. If nothing else, the process of answering this question might help highlight the absurdity in how we deal with problems. For example, if the problem has been keeping you occupied as I've already pointed out, then you've probably been investing energy in keeping the problem around, *not in solving it.*

If the problem is big, comfortable, and familiar, then it's incumbent upon you to change your attitude about whether your life is better served by what's comfortable or by what's challenging, exciting and stimulating. Answering the second question, in turn, gives you a head start on question number three:

If I'm not doing anything to solve the problem, why am I not doing anything to solve the problem?

The interesting revelation here is that companies tend to have the same problems that people do. Why? Because they're made up of people. A company doesn't desire a big comfort zone, protected and padded with old, familiar problems the way people do. However, when you pile a whole bunch of people into an organization, their collective comfort zones add up to one enormous problem-avoiding mechanism for the company.

Avoiding effort

One reason that personal problems or the problems of an entire organization go unresolved is because problem-resolution requires effort. Exerting effort, of course, is never as comfortable as coasting. If a problem is of any appreciable size, effort will always be required to resolve it. The only problems that require no effort to resolve are problems not worth worrying about.

I never fail to ask company leaders what their companies' biggest unresolved problems are. Every one of them quickly gives me some kind of answer. Sometimes it's efficiency within the organization. Other times it's massive turnover in the sales department or difficulty holding on to talented people in other departments. No matter what the unresolved problem is, I follow up by asking *who* has been assigned the task of solving the problem.

It's amazing how many companies don't have anybody assigned to tackle their largest unresolved problems—or any major problems for that matter. Sometimes the company head will sheepishly acknowledge that there once was someone assigned to the problem, but that person quit and wasn't replaced. You would think that keeping big problems around was more important to some organizations than keeping good people.

As I mentioned, these company heads can identify their number-one problem. They usually admit to having a meeting sometime back where the biggest problems facing the company were identified and ranked in priority. When I ask what problem the company is currently working on, if any, I'm often told that they're working on number 10 or 12. I ask what's going on with one through nine only to find out that they're being avoided, ostensibly because they require too much effort to deal with.

Selling sonic booms

Those who have been in my seminars, heard me speak in other situations, or read my first book already know that I was the first "sonic boom salesperson" in the United States Air Force. The title and the activity itself emerged from my answer to the question, "What's the biggest unresolved problem in your fighter squadron?"

With the advent of supersonic fighters, pilots like me were dragging sonic booms all over the countryside and annoying just about everybody who heard them. People didn't like being awakened at 4 a.m. by plaster falling in their face or by their windows being broken. Farmers were convinced that their chickens would not lay eggs and their cows wouldn't give milk because of the noise. Exaggerated claims that sonic booms caused everything from headaches to infertility kept an angry public up in arms.

Although sonic booms were our number-one problem in a peace-time Air Force, at least for those of us who had to live around the folks with broken windows and cracked ceiling plaster, I was embarrassed to admit that we were making no effort to resolve the problem. I felt a twinge of guilt as I told the fellow who had asked the question that we were trying to *learn to live with the problem.*

How many times have you said that to yourself in the course of your personal and/or professional affairs? Learning to live with it is a cop-out if there ever was one. It's ridiculous. So, I went out and spoke to hostile audiences as a representative of the United States Air Force, explaining why sonic booms were our edge against communist aggression and other threats to our national security. I called my 30-minute speech, "Better Boomed Than Bombed."

I created the job and filled the vacancy. The Air Force was only too happy for me to help get angry citizens off its back. The base switchboards had been lit up almost constantly since supersonic testing had begun. In a lesson that would help me become a successful corporate leader in the years that followed, I learned to turn adversity into opportunity.

My speaking challenges were opportunities for creativity. I would dress up in my "go-fast" suit with all of my medals proudly displayed across my chest. They were E.G.O. medals (In Air Force lingo, E.G.O. means "everybody got one." But civilians didn't know that.) If you think that you've sold a product or service with a high objection factor, you've never tried to sell broken glass and cracked plaster. Whereas, I could dazzle my audiences in the beginning, they started to realize about halfway through my presentation that the sonic boom salesperson on the platform in front of them was also a sonic boom *distributor.*

When I saw the countenance of the audience begin to change. I shifted gears and appealed to their patriotism and sympathy by describing how I took my little body, strapped it into a 70-foot-long, 22-and-a-half-ton jet fighter, lined up that aircraft on a windswept, ice-slicked runway in the middle of the night with less than one-sixteenth mile visibility, jammed the throttles forward, lit both afterburners, and felt 79,000 horsepower and 39,000 pounds of thrust flatten me against the seat back, rocketing down the runway from zero to 200 miles per hour in 13 seconds, climbing from sea level to 35,000 feet in 92 seconds, traveling 1,200 miles per hour, 20 miles per minute, flying that aircraft to the ragged edge of uncertainty, staring across that chasm into the face of the grim reaper, and laughing defiantly because I knew that I was helping to make the world safe for democracy.

That got them on their feet. For a moment, the farmer forgot about his chickens and the homemaker forgot about sweeping up broken glass and fallen plaster. Of course, I knew the rest of the story that they didn't know. As I accepted their thunderous applause, I knew my ritual instructions to my radar observer in the rear seat. I would say, "If you ever hear me give the order to eject, don't say, 'huh?' because you'll be talking to yourself."

The moral of my story is that working on your biggest unresolved problem can, and usually does, demand creativity and innovation. When people access their creative and innovative juices, they become energized. A burst of creative and innovative energy is the best butt snapper I've ever seen. Now that you know that taking on your biggest unresolved problem can be your biggest opportunity, you can stop avoiding it.

When folks refuse to tackle their biggest unresolved problems because the effort required seems too high of a price to pay, I often ask them what it is they're saving their precious effort for. None of us carry over unused effort from one day to the next. On the other hand, we can make tomorrow more effortless by working hard and smart *today*. Thomas Edison put it like this:

> *The reason a lot of people do not recognize opportunity is because it usually goes around wearing overalls looking like hard work.*

Well said.

Get after it

If you are feeling frustrated because you think you've engaged in problem-solving and no solutions are forthcoming, it's probably because you're wasting time looking for a *no-effort* solution. When you bear down and get after a problem, no matter how large, you are going to make progress. The satisfaction that comes from moving a mountain, even just a little, is far superior to the frustration of still scratching your head, some time later, in search of the mythical *effortless way*.

Caution!

Many people say to me, *"Danny, you just don't understand."* They go on to explain that they've never been any good at goal-setting and that it's never worked for them. These people are caught in their own trap. The fact is, they *are* setting goals. Worry itself is a goal-setting process. It's the ability to create vivid mental pictures of things *not wanted* but that will, with no doubt, be achieved because of misguided concentration.

In other words, what we vividly picture in our minds is what our energies are ultimately committed to achieving. Our minds are essentially saying to us, "You've been spending so much time thinking about this it must be important, so here it is for real. You've got it."

Obviously, visualizing a positive goal, the way things *should* be in the best of all possible worlds, dedicates your natural energies to making that image a reality. I don't mean to reduce the entire concept of positive thinking to a couple a paragraphs, but the fact is that it's pretty simple. If you're thinking about anything at all, it's got to be something you want or something you don't want. Make it your personal rule to concentrate on what you *want.* Focus on the positive.

Much of the goal-achievement process depends upon the developed powers of concentration. Therefore, the high-performance person lives *intensely in the present.* These people's lights are on and they're *home.* Spending the majority of your time in the past or the future distracts you from the effort that's required right now to resolve problems and clear the decks for better things to come.

People who dwell on the future might consider themselves visionaries. But they'd better have some dutiful and energized folks around them to deal with the *now* if they ever expect to reach the future, much less influence it. The excellence of our efforts in the present sets the stage and the tone for the future. After a seminar for hotel executives, Joe Topper, of Red Lion Inns, came up to me and said that he is committed to being an "island of excellence" in the pursuit of his career goals. What a great picture he drew. Being an island of excellence in the past or somewhere in the future has nothing to do with *now.*

Excellence is only effective in the present. All the goals in the world are meaningless unless you're living fully in the *now.* Deciding *not* to have a specific goal *right now* is a specific goal. If your goal is to not have a specific goal, then you've achieved it. You might feel empty and listless, but you've achieved your goals.

Breaking through

All of the pep talk and methodology in the world won't move you an inch until you invest the energy. I've described how making the solution to your biggest problem your number-one goal will energize you. I've thrown out some probing questions designed to bring you face-to-face with your true wants and desires as well as the courage of your convictions.

You can read through this stuff and nod your head as you turn the pages. You can feel yourself swell up with resolve to use this information and *get after it* like never before. You can put this book down and forget about everything you read within 30 minutes. Unfortunately, the latter is the most common course among those who give lip service to change.

To experience the exhilaration of *breaking through* your self-imposed barriers and experiencing life from the other side, you must dedicate yourself to a high-performance lifestyle not once, but every day and, often, numerous times throughout the day. As a final example of how you can emerge from your moment of truth and realistically expect to achieve all that you're capable of, I give you Mary Lawrence.

The Mary Lawrence story

Of the many people I'm proud to call my friends, my former employee, Mary Lawrence is among the most inspiring. The description of her turning point might be more vividly definable than yours, but it was no less critical to the impressive achievements in her life than your turning point or moment of truth will be to the quality of your life from this moment on.

Long before I met her, Mary was no stranger to tragedy. By her own admission, the five years following her husband's death had been a time of existing with little real direction in her life. She was a lonely and discouraged lady the night a driver ran a stop sign and left Mary's body tangled in the twisted rubble that was once two automobiles.

When the police and ambulances arrived, they discovered her motionless form. She later learned the ambulance attendant who found her said, "Get the rest of them first, she's already dead." By Mary's own account, an unconscious will to live was already building within her. In her unconscious state, she was facing a moment of truth—the first of many turning points to come.

In the ambulance, one of the attendants detected a faint pulse. No one's really sure why the attendant checked her, but her heart was refusing to quit. When doctors examined her at the hospital, they offered no hope for her survival through the night, much less any type of recovery. They felt that her facial and head injuries were too massive. What they didn't realize was that her unconscious will to live was becoming massive as well. Her spirit hadn't received a *scratch*.

With each passing day, Mary became stronger—not appreciably stronger, but stronger just the same. She knew what her biggest unresolved problem was and every ounce of energy she had was dedicated to living. She maintained her resolve in light of the fact that nobody predicted that her life, if she survived at all, would be anything more than a vegetative existence with tremendously impaired mental functioning.

Her facial bones and jaws remained wired together for months as she existed on a liquid diet. Doctors explained to her that, if she were to recover, they would have to perform two major reconstructive operations on her face, neither one of which could be done with the aid of anesthetics. Mary's reply to their warning was, "Let's get started."

During the protracted surgical experience, which included 15 root canals in addition to the reconstructive surgery, she learned more about the limits of human endurance than most people could ever know. During the long, painful months of recovery, Mary adopted the motto, "I can," as the most basic tasks became monumental for her broken body.

Emerging from the hospital one year later, she began to fully understand how different her life would be from then on. People she knew well couldn't recognize her face, still swollen a year after the accident. Some simply turned away, unable to look at her. But what caused Mary the most alarm was her loss of memory. She could no longer command her brain to remember names or thoughts. Somehow, she heard that studying for a real estate license was extremely difficult and required detailed memory work.

Anyone who knows Mary Lawrence isn't surprised to hear that the next thing she did was begin studying for a real estate license. She chose the hardest path available, not the easiest. She purposefully chose an activity that required an excessive amount of effort. Mary had to read each page of the complex text 50, 60, even 70 times just to reach a normal retention level. She made it her goal to solve the biggest problem confronting her and succeeded, not only in passing her licensing exam, but passed *on the first try*.

Mary came into my life after she had worked briefly for a couple of real estate offices without much success. It seems that working with the public was a bigger challenge than even getting her real estate license. The first two offices she worked for weren't able to provide her with the support or encouragement she needed to get a foothold in the business. Bosses told her again and again she couldn't cut it.

When she called me, she had already been through numerous moments of truth and each time refused to turn away from her goal. I'm sure that every time she "failed" in a new office, every instinct within her must have said, "Quit. Why put yourself through any more of this?" Nevertheless, she called because she heard that my company was opening a new office and she wanted to try again.

Her deliberate manner of speaking, necessitated by her memory problem was what first *appealed* to me over the telephone. We brought her on board and it quickly became obvious that Mary had learned much from her previous experiences. We put her in our sales training class and within months she became one of our outstanding first-year salespeople.

I thought Mary had climbed her mountain when she was recognized as one of the top 10 rookies of the year. As I presented her award at the annual awards dinner, she said to me, "Danny, save a place for me. I'll be back for an award again next year as a member of the Million Dollar Club." Even for someone without the setbacks that she had faced, entering the elite Million Dollar Club was an ambitious goal, to say the least.

The next morning, Mary bought a beautiful pink evening gown to wear a year later at the next awards dinner and hung it in. the center of her closet. She set a goal to maintain or even exceed her performance level for an entire year. Seeing the pink gown in her closet every day helped Mary visualize wearing it as she walked on stage the following year to accept her award. One of the greatest lessons Mary had learned was that she faced her personal turning point *every single day.*

Most people would have resolved to repeat a good performance in the exhilaration of the awards dinner only to drift away from the commitment as daily problems came up and obstacles got in the way. Not Mary. She faced a personal moment of truth every day and decided, all over again, to take the hard road to success. She knew that what she had almost lost was more than just being alive. What she had almost lost the night of her near-fatal accident was the *opportunity for self-determination.*

Needless to say, one of the proudest moments of my life came a year later, when I introduced the members of the Million Dollar Club. In the year that had transpired, I learned, for the first time, the *full story* of what Mary had gone through. Mary was not only a new member of our company's Million Dollar Club, but was our office's sales leader in all four categories.

Mary came on stage to accept her award wearing the beautiful evening gown she had looked at in her closet every morning for a year. She seemed to float across the enormous dance floor at the Disneyland Hotel amidst a standing ovation. "Climb Every Mountain" from "The Sound of Music" was playing and there wasn't a dry eye in the house. When I handed her that big trophy, she leaned over to me and said, "I told you I'd be back."

Spotlight on you

As the old sayings go, *You don't know what you've got until it's gone,* and *You never appreciate what you have until it's taken away.* How can those of us who have not faced the loss of everything worldly, as Mary did, know how valuable our life, and its potential, can be? I don't recommend going out and having a near-death experience. The most effective method is to continue taking fearless personal inventories. That means more questions.

Questions are only as useful as you are committed to answering honestly and reflecting on those answers. I suggest that you pause and *write down* the answers to the following questions and any other self-examination questions you read in this book. It's too easy to give a flip answer, flip the page and keep reading. It's not the following sleepless-night questions that will disturb your sleep. It's the *answers*. These are not questions to ask yourself some night when you have insomnia. These are questions to ask *tonight* to give yourself insomnia. If you ask yourself these questions, answer them, and then doze off, you didn't answer honestly. The first step to giving these issues focus in your life is to write them down. Etch them into your brain and begin developing a new context for the way you spend each day.

Sleepless-night questions

1. If I had to describe myself in three sentences, what would I say?
2. Each person I meet today takes my measure but, more importantly, how do I measure myself?
3. How much of my potential have I developed?
4. How much more of my potential will I have developed a year from today?
5. What's my plan for making that happen?
6. What extra effort am I willing to make today to launch my plan?
7. Will I make the effort?
8. What *mind games* do I play to convince myself that today does not matter and I can do today over again?
9. Is the high point of my life a past event or something I have carefully planned for the future?

10. Do I spend more time thinking about the past than I do planning my future?

11. The quality of my future lifestyle depends upon my current time habits. What can I expect from my future lifestyle?

12. I'm living my life in 24-hour segments. Which of my accomplishments of the past 24 hours am I most proud of?

13. Do I really believe that my success depends totally on me?

14. When I feel a rumble, even thunder in my heart, what am I willing to do to keep it there?

15. Will I do all that I am able to do to insure the achievement of my desired rewards?

I constantly ask myself, "Will I be like Mary Lawrence? Will I face my own personal moment of truth each and every day? Will I set goals? Will I keep my goals in sight every day? Will everything I do today improve tomorrow?" I know I *can* if I will:

1. Accept responsibility for how good I can really be.

2. See my goals as attainable.

3. Visualize the personal benefits that extra effort will bring.

4. Remain flexible and embrace change.

5. Anticipate success rather than fear it.

6. Identify what I really want.

7. Identify the *cost*.

8. Be willing to pay the price.

9. Start paying the price *now*.

10. Separate my goals into *financial, lifestyle, and personal growth*.

11. Make my goals *realistic, measurable, challenging,* and therefore *achievable*.

12. Make my first goal the solution to my biggest
    unresolved problem.
13. Concentrate on the positive results I seek.
14. Live intensely in the present.
15. Commit myself to a goal.

High-performance people see the future almost as clearly as they see the present moment. Their energy level is high because anticipation is the appetizer for accomplishment. It was Elbert Hubbard who said, "We can achieve what we can conceive." The 19th-century author also said, "Success is the realization of the estimate you place upon yourself." I would go on to add that you place a value on yourself and your potential in your moment of truth.

Developing Strengths

"To be nobody but yourself in a world which is doing its best, night and day, to make you everybody else means to fight the hardest battle any human being can fight and never stop fighting."

—e.e. cummings

Many an author, lecturer, and/or business consultant has trumpeted the virtues of goal-setting without providing the rest of the story. Many an individual comes out of a seminar or closes a book feeling as if setting a goal and realizing its accomplishment are one in the same. Many an individual is disappointed when s/he learns that setting goals and reaching goals are two entirely different processes.

In the *high-performance process,* goal-setting is one of the easier tasks, even though no task is fairly described as *easy* when we set out to change our behavior patterns. One of the most common experiences nearly all human beings share setting and *not* actively pursuing goals. We are all eager believers in the mythology of miracle cures. Even when we know better, we would still *like* to believe.

As much as we would like to believe that the mere act of setting goals would somehow guarantee that the goals would be attained, it doesn't work that way. That's probably why most diets fail. It's not the intention to do, but the doing itself that gets the job done. Intending is always easier than doing. Just willing something to get done won't budge the real world one inch.

Emerging from your personal moment of truth with realistic, measurable, challenging and exciting goals in the financial, lifestyle and personal growth categories simply means that you've set the stage for the next step in your personal *high-performance process*. The next component you need is a realistic inventory of your strengths. Everyone has strengths. Are you familiar with yours?

Out of the fire

Just like the blacksmith strengthens iron by repeatedly heating it and pounding it on the anvil, so too are human beings strengthened by the fire of adversity. Few concepts are more universally accepted among the many races, creeds, and cultures around the world. Somerset Maugham said it this way: "Adversity puts iron in your flesh."

Primitive tribes have historically made their prospective warriors endure tremendously difficult (and usually painful) rites of passage to prove their mettle. Initiation rituals for all manner of society and organization are designed to prove worthiness through the ability to successfully negotiate rigid tests of spirit and will.

Christian scripture, in both the Old and New Testaments, is replete with examples of how individuals become stronger and refined through adversity. To one degree or another, everyone has been tested by some sort of struggle in life. Although none of us looks forward to adversity, 99 times out of 100, every one of us is emotionally stronger for it in the end.

It's also healthy to get right down to business in our lives with the understanding that it ain't gonna be easy. Like Fred Allen says, "The world is a grindstone. Life is your nose." There are no teachers's pets in the classroom of experience. Comedian Louie Anderson once said, "Anybody who's had an easy life doesn't have anything to say that I want to hear."

No matter who says it or how, the point is always the same. The school of hard knocks will turn out students who are better prepared to succeed than the school of comfort and charm. Those with character strengthened by adversity will be able to penetrate and/or overcome obstacles that those with easier lives will bounce off of.

There is always luck to contend with. Just don't count on it. Follow J. Paul Getty's formula for success:

1. Rise Early.
2. Work Hard.
3. Strike Oil.

When you are committed to the *high-performance process,* you'll be extra appreciative when luck pays a visit. If you rely on luck or someone else's efforts to get you somewhere you'll be bitter and resentful when either or both are in short supply. It's not so much about being lucky as it is about being in the right spot when luck arrives—and being in the right spot has nothing to do with luck either.

If you want to calculate the riches of your life, don't recount every time you got lucky or that somebody bailed you out. Look back on times of adversity and challenge because those were the times when your strengths were being developed and refined. To inventory the areas in which you're truly skilled, look to your *experience.* Even more than training, it's experience that makes you good.

What you have when you have nothing

One of the finest speakers on the circuit these days is Charlie Plumb. Charlie was a prisoner of war in North Vietnam. When Charlie comes on stage, he puts two chairs a couple of feet apart and paces silently between them. The audience is riveted by his solemn, rhythmic pacing. Finally he speaks and explains that, for over six years, he paced in a North Vietnamese cell, less than three feet wide.

On the day he was shot down, he left the world he knew behind on the aircraft carrier and entered the prison with only his tattered flight suit. He had nothing. Or did he? With the audience's help, he begins to list what he had with him as he was captured. His ability to think, to remember, to reason. He had skills and knowledge. He had courage, creativity, and imagination.

As the list gets longer, it's increasingly apparent that Charlie had much more than his tattered flight suit when he entered that prison cell. So it is with your strengths. There is a lot more than meets the eye. When you feel like you have nothing to offer yourself or anyone else, you're just not looking deep enough.

It's in there

When people come up to me and say that they're facing what seems to be an insurmountable problem, I ask them if the current problem is the biggest or toughest one they've ever faced. "Oh, no," they reply. "This one is nothing compared to *that* problem..." These folks soon learn that if they treat their current problem with the same perspective that their larger problem required, the current problem suddenly seems far less ominous and foreboding. The net result is that these people instantly unleash problem-solving energies that they weren't aware they possessed.

You and every person around you have problem-solving skills and energies that are directly proportionate to the amount of adversity each has experienced. It's not that everyone exploits or is even aware of those hidden resources by any means. That's why it's imperative at this stage of your personal *high-performance process,* to call up those strengths and put them to use.

There's a *Broom Hilda* cartoon hanging on the wall above my desk. The cartoon, featuring the comical little witch, impressed me so much that I spent $50 to have it custom-framed. The whole Sunday paper only cost a buck. Actually, Broom Hilda herself is not featured in this particular cartoon. Instead, her troll-like, naive, innocent, little friend, Irwin, puts on a long-tailed formal tuxedo jacket, picks up a conductor's baton, and walks into the woods alone.

Irwin steps up on a fallen tree trunk and begins to wave his arms as if to conduct. There are no musicians, only rocks, trees, and flowers. Soon, musical notes pour from the rocks, trees and flowers and fill the panel. Finally, Irwin turns and confidently says to the reader, "It's all in there, you just have to work at getting it out."

The problem word once again seems to be "work." I swear there would be more people praying if they could only find a softer place to kneel. I meet a lot of people who are all set to hitch their wagon to a star—just as soon as someone hands them a star. Once each of us accepts that problem-solving, goal-achieving energy and talent exists within us. All that's left is the "work" required to reveal it.

It doesn't happen automatically. As always, traveling the hard road requires a conscious, informed choice. The decision to travel down easy street tends to come more effortlessly. Unfortunately, easy street doesn't go anywhere and you always end up no farther than where you started. Except in the rarest of circumstances, those whose success you admire only got there through tremendous, conscious effort.

Undeveloped strengths

In the overview of this book, we talked about how exercising previously undeveloped strengths pushes back self-limiting boundaries in your life. You're now learning where to find and how to identify those hidden strengths. Now that you know they're there, you can get past the wondering stage and expect to find substance within.

Take time to reflect on your life and its most challenging problems, even from your youth. How did you overcome those problems? Did you overcome them or did you just learn to *avoid* them? What problems have you successfully resolved? What's the biggest one? What types of problems can you solve well and often? The answers to these questions will serve as a window into your untapped reservoir of undeveloped strengths.

Your personal charter, at this point, is to do the very best that you can with the strengths available to you. Anything less is unacceptable.

> *"Few people during their lifetime come anywhere near exhausting the resources dwelling within them. There are deep wells of strength that are never used."*
> —Rear Admiral Richard Byrd

There's no excuse for not realizing your full potential once you've discovered the secret cavern in which all of your undeveloped strengths are hidden. The business you need to focus on is the development of your *undeveloped* potential.

Returning for a moment to that personal-potential thermometer we talked about in the overview, it's important to understand that the fuel you have to burn in order to make that temperature go up is your woodpile of undeveloped strengths. If you have honestly answered the questions, "Where is the mercury in my thermometer?" and "Where do I want the mercury level to be a year from now?" what's left is the task of heating up the mercury using your undeveloped strengths as your source of energy.

A year from now, if the mercury level is the same as it is today, then it's safe to say that you've not put any of your undeveloped strengths to work. I've already covered many of the reasons why we often avoid stepping up the development of personal potential. With these reasons in mind, you can no longer claim that you don't know where your strength is going to come from. Your stash of undeveloped strengths has been found.

Recipe for failure and frustration

Undeveloped strengths mixed with laziness. That's it. When we refuse to exert the energy to drag wood from the woodpile to the stove, the stove goes cold. Knowing that we're frustrated and unsatisfied with a cold stove, you might wonder why we sometimes let the fire go out. The answer is laziness. A cold stove, as useless as it may be, is sometimes preferable to the cost of stoking the fire. Preferable in terms of our anti-work, lazy side, that is. Letting the fire go out is never preferable in the long run.

No one can guarantee success. However, no effort to determine or develop personal strengths, usually out of laziness and/or lack of motivation, will virtually guarantee failure and frustration. A man recently won a bunch of money on a $1 lottery ticket. This was a poor man. He was so poor, you have to spell "poor" with four or five o's to get the picture. And he won a *bunch* of money—bunch with a capital "B."

This man quickly squandered his winnings on gambling and fast women. A curious journalist asked him why he spent all of his newfound wealth so quickly. The reporter wanted to know what was so attractive about poverty that made him want to return to it as soon as possible. The man simply replied that, because the small fortune he won only cost him $1, he didn't feel it was worth any more than $1.

Strange thinking when it's put that way. But we all have our moments when we apply some of the screwiest logic to the most straightforward situations. The man who won the lottery didn't search for the inner strengths that might have changed his life for the better. He relied upon the outside phenomenon of free money to improve his life. He took the easiest road and the lack of substance eventually caught up with him. He left his strengths undeveloped and wound up frustrated.

The mountaintop interlude

The mountaintop interlude is simply my name for the time you set aside for doing the reflecting I've been talking about. It could be the "creek-through-the-pasture interlude" or the "day-at-the-beach interlude." It really doesn't matter. I'm a great believer in the thought that, if we're going to learn anything about ourselves, we must spend some time alone, away from the distractions of others, including family. We're all too willing to be distracted by others when we need to focus on our own issues.

When I faced some of the most critical situations in my career, I went to the beach. There was an instinct that urged me to just dig in and work harder. Fortunately, I knew by then that just doing more of the same old stuff that got me in trouble to begin with would only dig me in deeper.

The best definition of insanity I've ever heard is, "Doing the same wrong thing over and over, and expecting a different result each time." I can't tell you how many times I've acted insane and I'll bet you've done the same thing a few times yourself. The crazy part is that we all go back and do it again—something that we already know doesn't work. A sign of real growth and maturity is developing the ability to catch yourself and change course before going down that same old road for yet another time.

> *"Everybody is a damn fool for 15 minutes every day. The trick is to not exceed your limit."*
>
> —Elbert Hubbard

My search for sanity through those mountaintop interludes is strictly a solo affair. My family doesn't go with me. Solitary thinking and reflection means *alone.* By going away from the problem and not getting buried deeper underneath it, I was better able to draw a perspective that helped me *solve* it. Most important of all is that genuine solitude allows me to clear the decks and go below to see what's in my personal hold.

It's the application of your undeveloped resources to the problem at hand that will produce the solution. Only when you can get an uninterrupted view of yourself can you properly scrutinize your undeveloped resources. Unleashing that untapped energy and creativity can't be done when your focus is on other people and other things.

I'm not suggesting that you retreat to some desolate place and contemplate your navel for the rest of your life. Getting alone and reflecting honestly and thoroughly on the experiences in your life that have strengthened you is only appropriate when you intend to move above and beyond where you are at the moment. It doesn't require a crisis. Tapping your own hidden resources is a means of self-empowerment that leaves you with a desire for more, and what you uncover and develop can help in most any aspect of your life.

Insight produces a change in self-expectation. Self-expectation is not limited to any singular situation, although it might start somewhere or be inspired by something specific. With elevated self-expectation will come a new perspective on everything you do. Peter F. Drucker said, "When you focus on a strength, it puts a demand on performance."

Curiosity and courage are the batteries that power your inner searchlight. Curiosity asks, "What have I not yet developed about myself that would benefit me?" Courage empowers you to use your new information once it's discovered. The following list suggests some of the discoveries you can expect to make during your own mountaintop interlude. The list with your name on it is as long and complex as your experiences have been to this point in your life.

Personal discoveries

I chose to begin the *strengths* section of this book with the e.e. cummings quote about individualism because strengths are highly personal. As I've already described, it's what's inside of you that determines your potential. In a world that throws images before us of what culture, commercialism or conventional wisdom regards as desirable, it's difficult to know where our own uniqueness stops and where the synthetic image begins.

For example, why do you want to be what you claim you want to be? Is it because that's where your unique strengths lead you or is it because you've been indoctrinated with what the media and social norms have preached as appropriate? There's nothing wrong with being a chicken farmer if you're good with chickens. If you're happier working on the farm, why are you pushing paper in an office building?

I'm not suggesting that everyone who reads this book drop his or her career and responsibilities cold and move to Newfoundland to write poetry. However, it's important that you be able to discriminate between what is in your personal arsenal of strengths and what's not. Time and time again, I meet people who tell me how frustrated and/or unsatisfied they are with their current job. They often feel stuck and unable to get ahead.

When I hear such complaints, it's a sure bet that these folks haven't engaged in sufficient self-discovery to appreciate their personal career composition. They haven't yet found out what they're uniquely good at or what their personal experience has prepared them to do best. Once you discover your strengths, don't be surprised to find out that the source of your greatest frustrations is found in your attempt to work in areas other than where your strengths are.

The following list of probable discoveries is by no means complete. It's simply a guide as you conduct your own self-inventory. The items I've listed will suit some better than others. The goal is to find what strengths are uniquely yours so you can use that information to sketch your own game plan for the future. Seek and ye will probably find:

1. Great storehouse of *tools* in the form of *talents*, *knowledge*, and *personal experiences*.

Talent

Each of us was born with certain talents. Although practice and refinement are required to maximize what might be called "natural" talents, each individual seems to be naturally inclined toward certain activities from earliest childhood. Some people are better with their hands, while others are better with their minds. Some people become painters and sculptors, while others become poets and composers. Some people are creative and expressive thinkers, while others are intensely analytical and number-oriented. Some people are talkers and some are listeners.

There comes a point at which acquired knowledge begins to shape, and possibly distort, natural talents and inclinations. I refer to the tendencies people have from birth as their natural talents, and the accumulation of what you've been taught by *others* as knowledge.

Knowledge

Of *talent, knowledge,* and *experience,* knowledge is the most questionable because it's what *someone else* thinks. Children are less equipped to discriminate between what's right thinking and what's distorted thinking. To the child, any adult has a certain credibility simply because that person is an adult.

Now that we're adults, we would hardly recommend to all children that they accept and adopt what any adult thinks merely on the basis of their being an adult. One of the signs of maturity is the ability to sift through the maze of contradictory thinking and develop a personal worldview and set of priorities. This is one of the reasons that I urge people to read and study as much as possible.

Reading and studying what others think is a terrific way to challenge your own thinking and also learn what thoughts are behind the great accomplishments you admire most in others. The key to your self-discovery process, as far as thinking is concerned, is to recognize which thoughts are truly yours as opposed to thoughts that you might have blindly accepted along the way, perhaps in your youth.

Many of the self-imposed barriers we face are constructed from thoughts and ways of thinking that are not helpful or that might even be negative or damaging. Just because someone else thinks something, that doesn't mean it's correct. Not all knowledge that we acquire though the years is helpful. Much of the knowledge we acquire needs to be dumped like ballast to lighten our load.

We have enough to deal with in life without adopting someone else's negative thoughts as our own. By the same token, much of the knowledge we can acquire by studying the thoughts of great and successful people can accelerate our quest for excellence. Talent refers to natural gifts, knowledge refers to acquired thoughts and both are filtered through personal *experience*.

Experience

Experience is the best measure of who you are. It's not the situations you find yourself in as much as it's what you choose to *do* in those situations that tells you what you're made of. Of course you're made of your talents and your thinking, however, it's how you *behave* in life that reveals to what degree you've allowed thinking to stifle talent or vice versa.

Experience is where the rubber meets the road in life. You can talk all you want about how you think and where you feel your talents lie, but I'll watch what you *do* if I want to get to know you. It's what you *do* and not what you *say* that opens the book on who you really are. If what you think and say you want in life are distinctly different from what you do, your self-examination isn't over yet.

Experience shapes and molds you according to how open you are to *learning*. To repeat yesterday and continue going down the same road-to-nowhere day-in and day-out is a surefire indication that you're not learning much from experience. For experience to be a positive tool in your life, you must learn from it and accept what your behavior says about your true intentions in life.

As my friend and creative-thinking mentor said:

> *We do what we are, we are what we think. What we think is determined by what we learn and what we learn is determined by what we experience.*
>
> *What we experience is determined by what we expose ourselves to and what we do with that experience.*

We all begin life with little or no control over our experiences. As we grow older, we gradually develop the capacity to get outside of ourselves and our circumstances and learn from them. Just like talent and knowledge, experience becomes a tremendous tool once you begin to learn from it and apply the lessons to your own *high-performance process.*

2. As enthusiasm builds, procrastination gives way to initiative.

Dam Busters

One of the most important reasons why goals need to be *exciting* is to invoke the positive benefits of enthusiasm. Where there is a lack of enthusiasm, all of your best-laid plans will get dammed-up behind the slightest obstacle. Enthusiasm is the dynamite that blows up the log-jam and gets you moving again.

Procrastination itself is the foreign object that blocks your flow. Whatever empowers an obstacle to bottle up your initiative is sure to be one of the many faces of procrastination. Usually it's fear that the successful outcome of some effort will make more demands on you than just leaving things the way they are.

Enthusiasm carries with it a healthy dissatisfaction with the way things are. That's why enthusiasm tends to keep things in motion and won't tolerate anything that bogs down the process. An office full of enthusiastic people is like a beehive. You don't need *butt snappers* because nobody stays in their seat for very long. Everybody is in high gear getting after something or other.

You get enthusiasm by witnessing the accomplishment of your daily goals, which are part of a larger plan. Notice I didn't say the accomplishment of your daily *tasks* but daily *goals*. When you're accomplishing daily goals, you're doing something new and not repeating another yesterday. When you're doing that, you can't help but be excited and enthusiastic.

Walk into an office without any enthusiasm and you're not going to see much movement. You can look at it the other way, too. Next time you walk into an office without much movement, note how much enthusiasm you can detect among the folks working there. I guarantee that you won't find much. Enthusiasm is the antidote for procrastination.

3. Control over attitude

In your intense self-evaluation you're going to discover something that surprises most people. Specifically, you have a great amount of control over how you *feel*. Attitude is the leading edge of how effective you are in life. If your attitude is such that you blame everyone and everything else for what happens to you, you're destined to fly in circles for the rest of your life.

Depending on the frustration level you feel as a result of the cumulative imbalance between *talent, knowledge,* and *experience,* your attitude might be only slightly out of adjustment or in self-destruct mode. In the early days of my business career, I could have made a list of the ways everyone around me was contributing to my lousy attitude. How about you?

Are you still laboring under the misconception that others determine your attitude? There's nothing like a time of solitude and self-examination to reveal that each one of us is in full control over our attitude. Other people can do many things to you, but they're powerless to determine how you're going to *feel* about it.

In the days when I would have rattled off a long list of names to describe who was in charge of my attitude, there would have always been one name conspicuously absent from every list—mine. Even if you're not willing to fully let go of the notion that others control your attitude, at least put your own name at the top of the list to give credit where it's due.

By doing this, you can focus all the blame you want on everyone else on your list after you've dealt with yourself. I don't think you'll find any need to waste your time blaming others for your attitude once you've confronted yourself. Regardless of your circumstances, it's your choice and your choice *alone* how you're going to feel about it. Once I learned that, I knew that a lousy attitude was only holding me back from enjoying my own *high-performance process.*

4. As performance increases, energy, and morale stay high.

What has self-examination got to do with increasing performance? Everything. You wouldn't be this far into the book if you didn't feel a real need to increase your personal effectiveness. The common belief is that energy and morale proceed high performance. Increasing performance pumps up energy and morale. They go hand in hand over time, but increases in performance will always result in increased satisfaction and enthusiasm.

There seems to be a natural connection between approaching the limits of your personal potential and happiness. People seem to be the least happy when they're nowhere near their potential. I've never seen a sad person succeeding at something that requires use of his or her natural talents.

Self-reflection will no doubt bear out that the times when you felt happiest and most fulfilled were the times when you had your natural talents, your knowledge and your background all lined up. If you're not sure of your natural talents, your acquired knowledge, and your library of experience, go to the times when you felt satisfied and excited about what you were doing. That was a time when your personal and unique combination of talent, knowledge, and experience was in alignment.

Upon reflection, it might seem as if such times of happiness and satisfaction happened purely by accident. They probably did. If you haven't before sought to identify your own unique composition, how could you have planned to match your activities with your personality?

After spending time in self-examination, enthusiastic pursuit of what interests you most will never again be an accident.

Coming down from the mountaintop

Time in solitude, self-examination, and recharged batteries prepare you for the next chapter in your life. As you come down from the mountains, home from the beach, or back from wherever you've gone to reflect, you bring with you a precious new understanding. You now know that it's not what you're doing that makes you miserable, it's not investing enough of *you* that makes whatever you're doing unattractive.

The whole point of learning who you are is to make it easier to inject more of what is uniquely you into your life. As I mentioned earlier, the commercial culture in which we live, critical parents and a host of other influences have probably distorted your self-image, if not completely annihilated it. Are you in a career that *somebody else* has convinced you to pursue?

Are you doing what you're doing because it's the only way you can afford to live in the house, drive the car, wear the clothes, or generally live the life that *somebody else* has convinced you is proper? If everything you do leads to the lifestyle that genuinely pleases you, you've somehow managed to align the talents, knowledge and experience that you went up the mountain to get in touch with.

The last thing I want to do is encourage you to become one of those "touchy-feely" creatures who can't make up their mind about anything until someone else gives them permission. But unless you discover who you truly are and what makes you tick, how can you make an informed decision to make anything truly yours? Increasing your level of sensitivity is valuable because your job as well as your life in general won't become truly *yours* until you discover and develop your unique strengths.

When you bring more of *you* to anything you do, you earn respect and admiration from others. When you see someone who's truly dedicated and passionate, you don't even have to agree with what they do to acknowledge that they at least deserve your respect for *fighting the good fight.*

You were built to be an original. Other influences have conspired since you were born to transform you into someone who was defined by what others think—usually for commercial purposes. Regardless of *why* others have felt compelled to shape your life, it's high time you take it back. In the end, it's not other people's attempts to shape your life that matters as much as how much you buy into it. Don't take this as an invitation to act irresponsibly.

If you're over 50 years old and 5'4" tall don't fight against your natural barriers and try to land that NBA contract. Self-examination is not intended to lead you into a useless battle against your natural limitations. In fact, quality self-examination will take you in the opposite direction.

Knowing who you are and what you're made of will serve to focus your energies more effectively on those things that you do best. Becoming a high-performance person means expending your energies in a more efficient manner than ever before. You can't do that by watering the milk or trying to make water flow uphill.

Creative people are unorthodox

Creativity is the opposite of conformity. There is a time for both. However, spending more time in conformity makes a dull boy. Spending 100 percent of your time being creative but irresponsible might land you in jail or, at least, have you living behind a dumpster. Whatever responsible balance you achieve, weight it on the side of creativity. If nothing else, being creative and a bit unorthodox will make you a more entertaining and fun person for the rest of us to be around.

Creativity is an indispensable component of the high-performance lifestyle. Creativity is defined as originality of thought and action. That's exactly what the *mountaintop* self-discoveries had in common. You are an original, unique in your thoughts and actions. To be a high-performance person, you can't escape creativity. It has to part of your unique and original composition as a human being.

The sucker hole

As I said, conformity has its place in a civilized society. In many ways, there is no more civilized society than the Air Force. The Air

Force is certainly well ordered, if not civilized. Nevertheless, I probably survived the Air Force because I never completely lost my uniqueness and the ability to break formation when the alternative was to become a smoking hole in the ground.

I once had a commanding officer who preached precision formation flying with a passion to behold. He hammered us with the concept of holding formation and following the formation leader no matter what. We were to do what the *lead* did without question. Responding to every move the *lead* made in flight had to become an instinct, not a choice.

I recall a classroom situation in which a young pilot asked the instructor, "What if the lead flies into a mountain?" The instructor thought for a moment and then turned to the young pilot. "I would want to see four equally-spaced holes along the cliff."

We're talking discipline here. The young pilot as well as the rest of us got the message. That message, along with as countless hours of training in precision formation flying, was etched into my brain one day when I was the third fighter in a three-aircraft echelon or *fingertip* formation. In a fingertip formation, a second airplane follows the lead plane to one side with less than six feet separating their overlapped wing tips. I was in the third plane and less than six feet separated my left wing tip from the right wing tip on the middle aircraft.

We were returning to base through some pretty stormy weather, maintaining our delicate spacing through severe turbulence at speeds around 500 miles per hour. I was paying attention. Our *lead* spotted a hole in the clouds below us and began a rapid descent. He was confident that the worst weather was behind us and he called the control center to cancel our instrument flight plan.

When flying under instrument rules (IFR), the air traffic controller, who monitors the aircraft on radar, directs aircraft. Canceling IFR means that you convert to visual flight rules (VFR) and the controller no longer provides separation and directional guidance. In short, you're on your own. As soon as our lead canceled IFR, we were eyeballing, flying by the seat of our pants.

Our lead, a very proud Air Force officer, fully expected to break out of the cloud cover as soon as we descended through the hole and make a VFR landing. He must have been surprised to find that the hole was a "sucker hole" meaning that what looked like our ticket to clear sailing was merely a passage to even more severe weather below. Indeed, the storm at the lower altitude was more violent than the one we just descended from. At moments like this I, the fighter pilot, used to reconsider the old adage, "If God had wanted us to fly, he would have given us feathers."

Trying to maintain formation, we were in the soup, flying blind with no air traffic assistance, getting knocked around as if we were in a cocktail shaker. I lost sight of the other two aircraft as we darted into thicker clouds. It was limited vision one instant and complete white-out the next. Still, our wing tips were only feet apart, Precision flying at all costs.

Then I lost sight of them again. The next thing I saw was the lead fighter and the number-two aircraft flying with their canopies about six feet apart. If this wasn't going to be a mid-air collision, it was going to miss a whale of chance. As we said back in the Ozarks of Southern Illinois, "It's better to say this is where he turned and ran rather than this is where he died."

I decided to become a nonconformist and do my world-famous *"let's get the heck out of here"* maneuver. I pulled the nose of my plane up, lit both afterburners and was gone in a hurry. I had decided there was a time and a place for everything and that moment was a time for breaking formation.

I say the lead *must* have been surprised by the severe weather waiting on the other side of the sucker hole because I never spoke to him about it. I found him at the Officers' Club, about a half-hour later, halfway through a bottle of Canadian Club. He didn't bring up the incident and, following his lead as I had been so strictly trained to do, neither did I. My lead and I had reached a convergence of natural talent (to be highly skilled, reactive pilots), knowledge (our endless training) and experience (near-death).

In the moment of crisis, we used our natural talents and instincts to throw the principles of formation flying out the window and successfully avoid the experience of dying in formation and crumpling a few million dollars worth of taxpayer-owned jet fighters in the process. At the critical moment, we acted as individuals, every man for himself, in whatever creative maneuver we could use to survive.

On creativity

"The man who follows the crowd, will get no further than the crowd. The man who walks alone is likely to find himself in places no one has ever been before.

"Creativity in living is not without his attendant difficulties, for peculiarity breeds contempt. And the unfortunate thing about being ahead of your time is when people finally realize you were right, they'll say it was obvious all along.

> *"You have two choices in life: You can dissolve into the mainstream, or you can be distinct. To be distinct, you must be different. To be different you must strive to be what no one else but you can be."*

—Alan Ashley-Pitt

Creativity, being the singular most dynamic component of the *high-performance process,* is worthy of your utmost attention. By developing as much of your untapped personal potential as possible, you will become a more creative person and more fun to be around. It will take doing some unusual and unorthodox things to develop what you've avoided developing to this point in your life. Creativity is the vehicle that helps you get inside of yourself to find out what you've got in there and how cleverly you can use it. (By the way, Alan Ashley-Pitt is the British-sounding pen name for Phil Wernig, a greeting-card entrepreneur from Santa Barbara, California, and a pretty creative guy.)

Creative people tend to have a more light-hearted perspective on life because they can rise above the rat race and see the humor in most situations. As you already know from your own personal preferences, someone who can find humor and maintain a healthy perspective is more enjoyable to be around than someone who is negative and tends to blow things out of proportion.

Characteristics of a creative person

As always, it's helpful to study those who have gone before. I've assembled what I believe are the traits of people who have demonstrated creativity in thought and deed throughout their private and professional lives. Those characteristics are:

1. Creative people have curiosity and a childlike sense of wonder.

There's a lot of talk these days about reconnecting with the child within us. Whether you agree with the psychological objectives of such a plan, it can't be argued that children have healthy curiosities. Through a child's eyes, the world is a fascinating place, constantly full of new discoveries and revelations. In our adult attempt to stay on the *grow,* what could be better than to reestablish the type of enthusiasm with which a child experiences the world?

Earlier, I described the need for two "C" batteries to power your inner searchlight. *Courage* was one battery, *curiosity* was the other. Without curiosity, what's going to inspire your search for hidden strengths and abilities? Without curiosity, what will motivate you to look beyond your present circumstances for any reason? Thank heavens people like Alexander Graham Bell, Madame Curie, Thomas Edison, Benjamin Franklin, Walt Disney, George Washington Carver, and so many others were *curious* people with a childlike sense of wonder.

If you've allowed yourself to become cynical and closed off over the years, it's time to restimulate your curiosity factor. Reading more, traveling, initiating discussions with interesting people you admire, and purposefully getting involved in new and unusual activities and hobbies are just a few ways to get your inquisitive juices flowing again.

Peter F. Drucker once suggested that you walk away from your situation, bend over and look back between your legs. He contends that once you look at a situation backwards and upside down, you'll have a more functional perspective, I can't think of one person or business that ever suffered from gaining a broader and more creative perspective. Besides, bending over and looking through your legs beats *eyeballing it* and *flying by the seat of your pants.*

2. Creative people are open to as many alternatives as possible.

People who are closed-off to new ideas and suggestions don't make many friends. They also don't make good bosses, employees, spouses, parents, teachers, etc. High-performance people are never threatened by new ideas. On the contrary, they encourage new ideas and outlooks. A high-performance person appropriates time to hear and absorb new and offbeat solutions.

Listening to and considering the new and unorthodox doesn't mean that you must act irresponsibly and do weird things just to call yourself creative and inquisitive. You might end up adopting very little of what you hear and learn. However, being open to the Earth-shattering proposal when and if it comes is how you make your own luck. As you know, people can't actually manufacture luck. Making your own luck refers to a manner of living that remains open and ready to great new ideas when they emerge. Being vigilant and prepared is impossible when your eyes, ears, and mind are closed.

3. Creative people constantly search for alternatives.

A creative person won't get trapped in narrow thinking. Sometimes we hear a new idea and jump on the bandwagon. That's good to a point. What if the new idea is not the best alternative? You have to be willing to consider other ideas. The fact that you backed a new idea to begin with is evidence that you're not afraid of change. So don't limit yourself. If one new idea is worth considering, then others are worth considering too.

There was once a pottery manufacturer in Ohio who realized he had a real bottleneck at the packing stage of his operation. He went into the plant to look things over and discovered that the pottery was being packed in newspapers. It immediately became clear to him that there's a natural tendency when working with printed material to *read* what's on the paper.

His people weren't sitting around reading newspapers instead of packing pottery. But they were sufficiently distracted now and then to slow the process down. Used newspapers were still the least expensive packing material he could get his hands on and he didn't want to buy more expensive packing materials, thereby adding costs to the operation.

He thought to himself, I wish these people could be blindfolded. So he did the next best thing. His solution: acquire *foreign language* newspapers that his people couldn't read. That's what he did and the packing operation returned to full speed. He looked for alternatives and found a good one.

4. A creative person is eager to test new ideas.

Even before a new idea is completely finished, refined, formulated, etc., it can be put before others for feedback and evaluation. A creative person does this because the input of others will no doubt have a beneficial effect on the quality of the idea as it reaches maturity. Keeping a new idea under wraps until it is unveiled as a new policy excludes most of what's good about the creative process.

Not only do people resent new ideas being forced upon them without the opportunity to participate in the development of the idea, it's possible that there was a better idea available that nobody got the opportunity to promote. Perhaps the new idea, once it's launched, proves to be a failure. The liabilities and vulnerabilities of the new idea could have been exposed in a less embarrassing development process that encouraged input from others. Creative people put new ideas out for maximum scrutiny as soon as possible in order to tune up the program.

5. Creative people develop comparisons to illustrate points.

It's not enough to simply speak in terms of numbers when portraying the probable outcome of a new idea. There's always more to an outcome than numbers. A creative person will adopt a metaphor or two to help others best get the complete picture. An increase of 100 percent, for example, is like doubling the sales. Doubling the sales is like shoving the throttle forward. Shoving the throttle forward places a bigger demand on manufacturing, etc.

In personal terms, learning a new word every day and using it in a sentence three or more times is like earning an advanced degree in semantics. Studying a new language means introducing an entirely new nation and society to your life. The creative person finds lots of comparisons and similarities to use in communicating ideas.

6. Creative people stay flexible at all times.

As I mentioned earlier, new ideas sometimes need to change direction, shape, size, and composition along their developmental path. None of that upsets the creative person. Although it's more convenient for new ideas to work perfectly the moment they're conceived, that rarely happens. A creative person will nurse a new idea along and make whatever investment in it that's required.

Part of remaining flexible is the willingness to abandon an idea if it proves unworthy of further development. Forcing a square peg through a round hole for the sake of pride is not the kind of attitude you'll find in a truly creative person. Creative people don't think in terms of failure, but in terms of learning from every experience. To the creative person a failed idea represents knowledge gained.

Becoming more creative

For those who don't feel creative at all but want to, as well as those who want to stimulate even more creativity in their lives, there are a few steps that will help. You should be noticing by now that the ideas I'm setting before you all dovetail into one another. Once you're committed to the *high-performance process,* these ideas become second nature to you and feel natural.

For starters, the first step to becoming more creative is to *spend more time alone.* As I described in the section on solitude and self-examination, spending time alone is the best way to distance yourself from the contamination of interruption and distraction. You have enough of this every day, you receive extra points for trying to be creative in the middle of chaos, even though it never hurts.

Step two is to *dream with a purpose* during the day. It's possible to be too focused on your work and stifle any creative thoughts that might come your way. Notice I didn't say *daydream*. Clearly, it would be irresponsible to waste valuable time keeping your mind completely free for any errant idea that might pop into your head. The key to keeping your mind open and available to wander where your creative spirit leads is to identify times throughout the day when you can afford to dream of new high-performance ideas. A survey that appeared in the 1993 summer issue of *Exec* magazine revealed that 71 percent of the office workers surveyed reported they had, over the previous year, made at least one dream that occurred during the day become a reality.

Driving, walking, or getting a cup of coffee or a sandwich are all times when you can knowingly let your mind wander a little. Just sitting and staring out the window for a few minutes at various times of the day is well worth the time spent if you knowingly keep your mind available to new thoughts and information. There's no vice in letting your thoughts wander freely in the context of a productive day.

Step three is to *be gullible*. Be willing to stay with each new idea until you have a good, solid reason to reject it. Too many people choke the life out their own creativity by discounting new thoughts and ideas too soon. To reject something out of hand just because it doesn't make *complete* sense at the moment is to potentially forfeit what might materialize into a tremendously beneficial concept if given sufficient time to ferment.

Step four is to *allow yourself emotional conflict*. Emotional conflict or uncertainty is the genesis of creativity. If an idea seems unsettling to you, there might be a good reason. If a new thought shifts your load a little, chances are good that you're really on to something. When something makes you uneasy, it's time to do something about it, not ignore it.

The truly creative person lives to challenge old, staid beliefs and attitudes. If something pops into your head that makes you a little nervous, check it out. Grant yourself some creative free time to dig deeper and see what's going on. You could be missing a breakthrough idea by dismissing it simply because it makes you feel uncomfortable.

"Only those who attempt the absurd will achieve the impossible."

—Albert Einstein

Step five is to *assume that illogical thoughts have credibility.* To dismiss new thoughts just because they might not seem logical at first blush is to run the risk of throwing out the baby with the bath water. The fact is that you simply might not be prepared to receive the information. Who knows what mode your mind might be in when a stray thought happens by?

If you're busy working out of your analytical/linear left brain when a artful/aesthetic thought occurs, the new thought won't compute. That doesn't mean that the idea lacks value. When this occurs, jot the new idea down so that you can revisit it later when your more creatively right brain oriented. The once illogical thought might suddenly make all the sense in the world. I'm convinced that many terrific solutions to personal and professional problems are lost because they're not digestible the moment they arrive.

> *"Some of our best ideas have come from letting our engineers wander in where angels fear to tread."*
>
> —Henry Ford

The creative environment

What Henry Ford was talking about isn't as simple as it might seem. To this day, it's a rare company that makes a conscious and concerted effort to establish and nurture a creative environment. Why else would they send their executives away from the company campus to some resort setting to be creative? Creativity needs to be part of everyone's diet, every day. A high-performance person doesn't wait for a management retreat to be creative. S/he is creative day-in and day-out, awake or asleep. Creativity should be a way of life.

Business managers, employees, salespeople, teachers, parents, and anyone who can benefit from personal growth and the growth of others can't ignore their personal responsibility to encourage and support the creative process. The primary manner in which creativity can be encouraged and supported is to create and sustain an environment were creativity is applauded and rewarded instead of discouraged.

It's all too common for creative impulses to be criticized and even punished. The pattern often begins at home in early childhood and then continues through school and into the workplace. As I mentioned, there are times to conform and times to be creative. However, the balance between creativity and conformity can be tilted too far in favor of conformity if the parent, teacher or business manager seeks to maintain order at all costs.

Sam Walter Foss, who died in 1911, penned a rambling rhyme that truly captures the essence of mindless conformity:

One day, through the primeval wood,
A calf walked home, as good calves should;
But made a trail all bent askew,
A crooked trail as all calves do.
Since then two hundred years have fled,
And, I infer, the calf is dead.
But still he left behind his trail,
And thereby hangs my moral tale.
The trail was taken up next day
By a lone dog that passed that way;
And then a wise bellwether sheep
Pursued the trail o'er vale and steep,
And drew the flock behind him too,
As good bellwethers always do.
And from that day, o'er hill and glade,
Through those old woods a path was made;
And many men wound in and out,
And dodged, and turned, and bent about
And uttered words of righteous wrath
Because 'twas such a crooked path.
But still they followed—do not laugh—
The first migrations of the calf,
And through his winding wood-way stalked,
Because he wobbled when he walked.

This forest path became a lane,
That bent, and turned, and turned again;
This crooked lane became a road,
Where many a poor horse with his load
Toiled underneath the burning sun,
And traveled some three miles in one,
And thus a century and a half
They trod the footsteps of that calf.
The years passed on in swiftness fleet,
The road became a village street;
And this, before men were aware,
A city's crowded thoroughfare;
And soon the central street was this
Of a renowned metropolis;
And men two centuries and a half
Trod in the footsteps of that calf.
Each day a hundred thousand rout
Followed the zig-zag calf about;
And o'er this crooked journey went
The traffic of a continent.
A hundred thousand men were led
By one calf near three centuries dead.
They followed still his crooked way,
At least one hundred years a day;
For thus such reverence is lent
To well-established precedent.
A moral lesson this might teach,
Were I ordained and called to preach;
For men are prone to go it blind
Along the calf-paths of the mind,
And work away from sun to sun
To do what other men have done.
They followed in the beaten track,

And out and in and forth and back,
And still their devious course pursue,
To keep the path that others do.
But how the wise old wood-gods laugh,
Who saw that first primeval calf!
Ah! Many things this tale might teach,
But I am not ordained to preach.

We would do our children, our fellow human beings, our students, our employees, and ourselves, a better service if we acknowledged the value of creativity and invested the extra effort to make room for creativity in our day-to-day lives. For example, children should be rewarded when they discover a new and better way of solving a problem or accomplishing a task.

That might sound easy, but what usually happens is that parents and teachers reward children for falling into the line of conformity, even when they've been creative. To a child, discovering that s/he can do something that s/he could never have done before is an act of creativity. In fact, new and never done before is a good definition for creativity.

Learning the roles and rules of civilized people is important, but it takes some extra effort to make people of any age feel as if their productive behavior is part of their uniqueness and not a function of becoming like everyone else. In other words, even though we all do many of the same things, each of us has a unique way of going about it. That's the point we want to encourage in others and in ourselves.

By creating an environment that encourages and supports uniqueness, creativity becomes part of our lifestyle at home, at school, at work, and at play. The high-performance person seeks to maintain a creative flow in his or her life at all times. When creativity is part and parcel of your everyday affairs, life is never dull and it's usually much more productive. Creativity fuels performance by drawing constantly on that reservoir of undeveloped strengths that each of has within us.

Creativity flourishes in an environment of:

1. Experimentation.
2. Playfulness.
3. Spontaneous behavior.

Experimentation

When people try something that doesn't work, do you tell them that they screwed up? Do you say that to yourself? How many times have you heard a parent say to a child, "That was dumb"? It doesn't take a whole lot of effort to say "That didn't work. It's time to try something else." The latter comment carries an entirely different message.

The first comment means, "Don't try things that might not work or your intelligence will be questioned." Not many people are going to try new things when they can expect criticism. The second comment doesn't cast aspersions at the person who tried something new, it merely acknowledges that the experiment didn't produce the desired results. Such acknowledgment doesn't discourage another try.

In the classroom, the home, or the office, if experimentation is openly encouraged, there will be more experimentation.

Remember, behavior that's rewarded tends to be repeated. You can post notes on the refrigerator or the bulletin board that detail the problems that certain people are working on. Such a display of experimentation underway is a clear signal that experimentation is encouraged.

Your discussions should include mention of experimentation that you're involved in. Sharing ideas with others is always good practice. Discourse about experimentation is another way to send the message that creativity is a worthwhile and desirable part of day-to-day living. Both words and actions should be purposefully used to encourage experimentation.

Playfulness

That might sound childish at first, but remember that it's valuable to maintain a *childlike sense of wonder* about things. Someone who is constantly serious, with nose to the grindstone might *look* like the picture of dedication. In truth that person might be missing a great many creative solutions. Encouraging and maintaining an atmosphere of playfulness isn't difficult when dealing with children. With adults, it's a bigger challenge because so many people have been led to believe that playfulness is childish and immature. Some of the most productive offices I've ever seen go out of their way to make sure that the mood stays light and that there's humor everywhere.

Humor is one of the best ways to keep a healthy and productive perspective on things. Humor and playfulness go hand in hand. When the parent, teacher, or boss is a stoic old grouch, nobody else has permission to be funny. As with all things, there can be too much emphasis on humor at the expense of productivity. On the other hand, a lack of humor and lighthearted spirit will also have a detrimental effect on productivity. Keeping everybody around the office solemnly towing the line doesn't necessarily result in maximum performance. An environment of laughter adds a lot.

Spontaneous behavior

Rules and regulations should only exist to keep everyone in the organization pulling their oars in the same direction. *How* each person pulls his or her oar should be left to the individual as much as possible. As I've already discussed, the more uniqueness a person can bring to his or her tasks, the more personal energy will be invested.

No matter how many rigid rules and procedures an organization adopts, real life doesn't obey strict rules and regulations. I've seen companies that are so regulated that they begin to demand that their customers follow the company rules. Real life doesn't work that way and companies that try and impose their rigidity on the general public ultimately become flexible or go out of business.

People are spontaneous creatures by nature. Only when the spontaneity has been snuffed-out by an inflexible environment do people become dull. I've found that even the blandest personality has a lot of spunk if you coax it out. Maintaining a healthy balance of appropriate behavior at home, in school, or at the office is important. That means that spontaneous behavior should not only be allowed, but actually encouraged.

Let the spirit move you and those around you. When a great idea hits, don't waste time getting some feedback on it. When you see someone trying something risky, let that person know that you appreciate it. When someone's efforts don't produce desired results, go ahead and let that person know how much you appreciate the *effort*.

Give yourself all of this encouragement as well. When it seems like a good day to send the entire office to the beach, do it. Being spontaneous is a hedge against losing good ideas and emotional momentum. If someone in the office has a burning desire to work on this or that problem today, bend the schedule, change a few appointments and do whatever is necessary to exploit whatever creative burst of energy is taking place.

The same goes for you. When *you* feel like being spontaneous, there's generally a reason. It's probably your creative control center telling you that a solution is at hand and all you have to do is follow your creative impulses to access the desired results. You might not even know what the problem is when the solution pops out at you, but your spontaneous impulses will let you know that what you're coming up with is important.

The kaleidoscope approach

Like Peter F. Drucker's earlier suggestion to bend over and look at things from a backward and upside-down perspective, the *kaleidoscope approach* is a way of changing how things appear. Looking at life, problems and day-to-day activities as if they were tumbling in a kaleidoscope can present an endless parade of possible solutions. Make it a point to consider things from every angle you can think of, then turn the whole thing upside-down and repeat the process. Granted, most of the new patterns and arrangements won't result in higher performance. But it only takes one good solution to turn around a bogged-down operation or speed up a good one. Who cares how many times you tumble the kaleidoscope! The point is to *do it*.

What makes a new idea successful?

How do you know when a new idea is destined to be successful? There's nothing that beats experience to confirm the validity of a new idea. However, you can't try *every* new idea you come up with. There just isn't time. Spending all of your time testing new ideas would throw your productivity out of balance. You need to put new ideas through a screening process.

I've found that a simple, three-step examination that Walt Disney used is all you need to indicate whether a new idea should be taken to the next level. The three criteria are:

1. A successful idea must be unique.

If a new idea isn't sufficiently different than what you're currently doing, then the idea is probably a rehash of present policy. Doing more of the same is hardly a way to inject new thinking and enthusiasm into the process. The element of uniqueness stimulates a natural curiosity and heightened sense of anticipation to those involved with its implementation.

2. A successful idea must have an element of proprietary interest.

When people take a special interest in something, it becomes proprietary, or a part of them. When someone recommends a book, a movie, or a restaurant, it's because that person has taken a personal interest in it.

Word-of-mouth recommendations are the best possible type of advertising because a personal recommendation is genuine and not a ploy for commercial gain. When a new idea gains the proprietary recommendation of those involved with its implementation, it's because those people feel the idea will work in their best interest. If your interests are consistent with theirs, then a highly-endorsed idea should move to the top of your list.

3. A successful idea must have a flair factor. If it's worth doing, it's worth doing big, it's worth doing right, and it's worth doing with class.

A successful new idea deserves to be celebrated. After all, a good new idea will increase personal and organizational performance. If the new idea doesn't seem as if it's worth any fuss or special attention, perhaps it's not worth the effort. If the new idea is worth celebrating, the attention it's given will help promote it and get more people on the bandwagon earlier. A good new idea should excite everybody involved in its implementation.

The creativity process

There are four steps to the *creativity process*. As with any developmental process, it's important not to skip over any of the steps in the creative process. Failing to give new ideas sufficient scrutiny will likely result in premature implementation or premature abandonment. In either case, the new idea wasn't given the opportunity to increase performance.

Step 1: Preparation

If you're intent on solving a problem, you must prepare. Unless you make an attempt to learn what others before you have tried, you're doomed to cover the same ground they did. Thomas Edison was a good example. He spent a great deal of time studying what others had done with a concept before he would begin his own experimentation. He saw no value in repeating mistakes that others had made before. Edison saw more value in making new and creative mistakes that brought him closer to success.

Preparation means research. Another type of research is soliciting opinions on how a problem should be defined and how others think it would be best resolved. If there is consensus on certain unsatisfactory outcomes, then why waste time going down those roads? In the end, the net result of preparation is that the ultimate solution you devise will probably be largely comprised of elements that nobody had thought of before.

Preparation will get you closer to those undiscovered elements faster by saving the time and energy that would have otherwise been wasted retracing old efforts. This doesn't mean ignoring the findings of others. Certain components of the experimentation others have done might fit well into your puzzle.

Step 2: Incubation

Individual items in a delicious stew, if eaten raw, wouldn't have the same flavor or texture. Raw carrots, potatoes, celery, beans, and pieces of beef wouldn't be very appealing if they were mixed together but not cooked. The same is true of ideas. Good ideas are usually made up of smaller ideas that need to be "cooked" before they represent the usable idea—not to water them down or dilute them but to add synergy.

The incubation phase of the creative process is a time for patience as you observe how the various elements react to one another when combined at certain temperatures and in various proportions. If all the pieces seem to be there but they haven't jelled yet, you probably need to let them simmer a little longer.

When I'm in a problem-solving mode and run into a dead end, I back off and let things steep. Usually, I'm awakened in the middle of the night with the answer. When you see a high-performance person rush into the office early in the morning, s/he has probably been awakened in the middle of the night with a possible solution to that problem that was incubating. Believe me, when a solution is ready to emerge from a short, medium, or long incubation phase, it will let you know.

Step 3: Insight

After the idea has emerged from the incubation phase, everything looks much clearer to you. That's insight. When the answer looms vividly before you, don't get suckered into thinking that the creative process is completed. The clearly identified solution is now ready for the fourth phase of the process. Although the idea might appear to be a flawless solution, watch out. Looks can be deceiving.

Step 4: Verification

Is the idea really as good as you think it is? When we give birth to a new idea, we're naturally protective of it. After all, it's proprietary. Be careful not to put up a fence around your new idea and defend it to the death. For starters, if you act like that, others will withhold valuable feedback from you. Who wants to comment on a new idea if they're going to get their head bitten off?

When you're all pumped up about a new idea, the temptation is great to say, "Let's go with this immediately." Even when fast action is called for, a verification process is still a good safeguard against premature implementation and, possibly, the wasting of a good idea. The four-step verification process, outlined below, can be done quickly. However, the important questions it raises shouldn't be taken lightly.

1. Suitability. Will the new idea remedy the problem, be a *stopgap,* or a permanent solution?

2. Feasibility. Is it affordable and practical?

3. Acceptability. Will management and/or the customers go along with it? What positive and negative things will *each* of these groups have to say about it?

4. Improvability. The idea might be good now, but how will customers demand improvement over time? How can the idea serve as a springboard for improvements after being put into practice?

These questions all need to be answered on paper. You should always get input on these questions from a variety of sources to promote objectivity. Consider defining management and customers to best represent your situations. For example, to a teacher, management might be the school principal or the school board. Customers might be students and/or parents. Hearing negative feedback should be considered beneficial. Negative feedback gives you information that will help you *tune* the idea before it's put into motion.

Roadblocks to creativity

It should be obvious by now that creativity is a process. New ideas need to evolve. During the time that new ideas need to evolve, problems can arise that block the development. Some of the road-blocks are unpredictable and need to be dealt with as they arise. Other blockages are caused by preexisting conditions that can be addressed ahead of time.

Like barriers to personal growth and development, barriers to the creative process can be either natural or self-imposed. Besides the roadblocks that are beyond your control, the creative process can be encumbered by roadblocks that you erect yourself. Self-imposed barriers to the creative process can be conscious or unconscious, intentional or unintentional.

The following list of four primary roadblocks to creativity contains self-imposed barriers because those are the ones that you can minimize or completely eliminate through modification of your existing thoughts and behavior. It's not easy changing thoughts and behavior. You've been thinking the way you think and acting the way you act for a lot longer than you've been interested in creativity.

Roadblock 1: Habit

But we've always done it this way. This is still the mission statement of too many organizations that ought to know better. Saying that you've always done something a certain way is not the same as asking, "If it ain't broke, why fix it?" I'm not a big fan of the latter comment. But at least it acknowledges that something is working.

I frequently hear people defend traditional and time-honored methods *even when the methods don't work!* Habit and ritual seem to have a strangle hold on the productivity of many individuals and organizations. As I discussed earlier, human beings are creatures of comfort and comfort can be found in what's *familiar.* One of the main obstacles to the high-performance process is the desire to be comfortable at the expense of productivity.

Roadblock 2: Fear

Fear and creativity are mutually exclusive terms. They cannot exist in the same space. Fear is a real emotion and no one can make fear go away completely. However, fear should serve as the springboard to launch a search for solutions, not as the driving force. Where fear is left in charge, everything everyone does becomes avoidance. People's energies are used in *not* rocking the boat instead of moving the boat forward. I've seen people balk, saying, "The competition wouldn't like it." Can you think of a better reason to go ahead and do something?

You need to acknowledge those things that make you afraid. If you've done some honest self-inspection, you'll be aware of the things you fear and why. The good news is that fear, when brought out into the light of day, tends to dissipate. Only when fears are kept under pressure in dark, secret caverns deep within you, do they have such powerful influence over your thoughts and actions.

Where the development of new ideas is concerned, the poison gases that fear gives off can suffocate an idea before it's had a chance to mature. Fear avoidance is one of the human race's most ardent pastimes. Like the actor, Glenn Ford, told me, either you do the things you fear or fear is in charge. The high-performance person knows how important it is to get fear under control so that it doesn't take control.

Roadblock 3: Prejudice

One of my biggest frustrations, as I travel back and forth across America working with corporations, is hearing the same response to new ideas over and over again. "That idea sounds great, Danny," they tell me, "but it would never work here at our company." Prejudice. The prejudging of ideas without considering their individual merit.

Rigid and inflexible thinking, designed to preserve the established order of things, is prejudicial thinking. Prejudice has roots in habit, but more so in fear. People fear what they don't know much about. Yet, instead of reaching out and learning more to counteract their ignorance, they avoid it even more. It's a shame, but it happens all of the time. A high-performance person has no time or energy to waste on prejudice, just as s/he has no time or energy to waste on unimportant and petty considerations.

Roadblock 4: Inertia

When people ask, "What's wrong with the way we're doing it now?" What they're really asking is why they should start moving when they've been motionless for so long, or why they should chart a new course after so much time on their old course. An individual or an organization that makes daily sacrifices to the status quo is fighting nature. A good rule of thumb: *If it's been done one way for two years, there's an 80-percent chance there's a better way of doing it.*

You can't expect to get anywhere by repeating yesterday in a world that doesn't. The world of business in particular is increasingly intolerant of sluggish performance and resistance to change. Fortunes are being lost or, more appropriately, swept away by a flood of new thinking and initiative. The old maxim, "S/he who hesitates is lost" has taken on renewed meaning.

I did a program for a major industrial association not long ago and the national president made a comment during his speech that really struck home with me. He said that there has been more change in that industry over the past five years than in all the time before. I had already heard that the human race has acquired more knowledge since 1960 than from 1960 back to the beginning of recorded history.

There is simply no way that a person who seeks the benefits of the *high-performance process* can stay out of the information current. The constant flow of new information isn't going to slow down any time soon. In fact, it appears to be accelerating. The application of new information, guided by timeless truths, demands constant motion and defies stagnation.

Slaying the "idea killer"

Even when you get a new idea through the verification process, there might be some who will ask you to soft-pedal it. No matter how good an idea is, there will always be someone in the organization who insists on smothering it under a bureaucratic blanket. It might be professional jealousy or any number of other unfortunate reasons. But it happens. What can you do?

The answer is: Turn the *idea killer* into a valuable *devil's advocate*. Take up the idea with its principal detractor and ask what points about the idea the person likes. Try to get at least two or three positive comments. Then ask what the detractor *doesn't* like about the idea. Now acting as a helpful critic, the idea killer will highlight weaknesses in the idea that you need to address.

Once a person has said one or two positive things about an idea, the negative comments will be more objective and helpful. The comments that your chief detractor makes should focus your thinking on how to make your idea even more effective. Turning negatives into positives is a significant feature of a high-performance person. There is always some positive energy in negativism. The challenge is extracting it.

Maximizing a new idea

Even as new ideas are being developed, their horizons should be stretched. The world is full of useful products that resulted from attempts to solve problems that had nothing to do with the idea's ultimate application. Part of remaining open to new ideas is to remain open to new applications. In finding broader or different applications for new ideas, you can also recruit support from other sectors that wouldn't have had any previous reason to be involved.

> *Can the idea be put to uses other than the use it was originally deigned for?*
>
> *Can the idea be modified in any way?*
>
> *Can the idea be reduced in scale or expanded?*
>
> *Can the idea be upgraded?*
>
> *Can the idea be substituted?*
>
> *Can the idea be rearranged?*
>
> *Can the idea be reversed?*
>
> *Can the idea be combined with another idea?*

The following questions are a helpful final guide to making a go or no go decision on a new idea.

> *Does the new idea make better use of most peoples' time, talent, and energy?*
>
> *Does the idea improve operations or product quality?*

Does the new idea cut waste or unnecessary work?

Does the new idea improve working conditions and customer service?

Does the new idea represent the goals of the high-performance process?

A new idea doesn't have to solve the problems of the world to be worth a shot. As long as a creative new concept meets the criteria set forth, it's a valuable addition to your life. You will always have to use your best judgment and exercise discrimination. That's simply part of being a responsible person.

Creativity is critical to the *high-performance process* because it is the most effective mechanism to access your unique talents and abilities. Nothing is more central to the discovery and development of your undeveloped strengths than creativity. As Thomas Edison said, "The answer is out there. Find it." I say there's a great deal more inside of you than you're aware of. Find it.

Good news and bad news

Adversity lies ahead for anyone wanting to commit themselves to the self-discovery and strength development that the *high-performance process* requires. If it was easy, everybody would be a high-performance person and the world would be unrecognizable. It's a nice thought, but highly unlikely.

Even though every human being has undeveloped strengths and unrealized potential, high-performance people are few and far between. But that's an even greater motive to become one. Unclaimed opportunity is waiting for the few men and women who are willing to make the sacrifices the *high-performance process* requires. The effort necessary to develop your undeveloped strengths pales in comparison to the excitement of learning and understanding more about *yourself.*

Becoming a high-performance person and engaging in the strength-development that the process calls for means that you must seize on the best aspects of your character and build upon them. The balance in your life will shift away from negativism and toward a brighter, more positive outlook.

You will feel young again. It's true. One of the personal characteristics we most mourn the loss of is the optimism and upbeat, never-
say-die attitude of youth. If you feel increasingly cynical about life as
you grow older, it's because you've grown tired of the bumps and snags.
It's easier to build up a callus around your heart than to continue
risking rejection for the sake of some elusive goal.

Once you realize that the goal is inside of you in the form of undeveloped potential—completely under your control—attaining it becomes less threatening. How can anyone stomp out your desire to
know yourself better and mine the vein of precious undeveloped personal strengths? How many of your hidden strengths ever see the
light of day is up to nobody but *you.*

Planning for Performance

"Many people fail in life, not for lack of ability or brains or even courage, but simply because they have never organized their energies around a goal."

—Elbert Hubbard

Selecting desired rewards and setting goals establishes a target. Discovering and developing hidden strengths provides the tools for making the goal a reality. Planning for performance means setting a *strategy*. The plan you establish to reach your goals will serve as a road map that leads from where you are now to your desired rewards, using existing and newly-developed personal strengths.

Like goal-setting, planning requires focusing on the future. My good friend and mentor, James Newton, had the privilege of knowing Thomas Edison, Henry Ford, Harvey Firestone, Alexis Carrel, and Charles Lindbergh, all of whom were mentors to him. Jim describes how his mentors always focused on the future. Until the time of their deaths, they never ceased planning for accomplishment.

As with goal-setting and self-examination, planning can also become an endless treadmill used to avoid increasing personal performance. Planning needs to be used in concert with the first two steps in the *high-performance process* to keep you in motion rather than to provide you with another way to get sidetracked. The excitement of becoming uniquely you is key to keeping the planning phase in perspective.

With excitement and anticipation comes increased energy. Elbert Hubbard's quote at the beginning of this chapter well describes the value of focusing energy. In achieving goals, a wide variety of existing and newly developed strengths must be employed. Despite the best-laid plans, there are sure to be many twists and turns, victories and setbacks along the way. Focused energy will keep the ball rolling and your plan will be the focus of your energies.

Unimportant work

Many people do unimportant work very efficiently. Are you such a person? In the overview I listed 10 characteristics of high-performance people. The second characteristic is *high energy in an absence of pettiness.* Pettiness is mentioned in the same breath as high energy because unimportant things are the enemy of focused, productive energy.

High-performance people know the difference between what's truly important and merely interesting. I've always liked the analogy of rearranging deck chairs on the *Titanic,* after it had been struck by the iceberg. It seems to be a waste of time to any rational person. Nevertheless, in virtually every company and organization in America, somebody is intensely rearranging the deck chairs, seemingly completely oblivious to the more pressing issues at hand.

Getting caught up in minor, inconsequential stuff makes it appear as if we're engaged in work of tremendous importance when in fact we're merely busying ourselves with low-risk activities. Low risk because, the more inconsequential the issue, the less anyone really cares about the outcome. Rearranging deck chairs on a sinking ship is easy because the chairs are floating. In the same way, lining up paper clips in a failing business is easy because nobody cares about paper clips.

Expending energy on unimportant things is just our old nemesis, procrastination, popping up in another disguise. When we procrastinate, we're avoiding responsibility for *succeeding.* Making something happen runs the risk that things could improve. Making sure that you're not involved in anything of consequence guarantees that nothing will change—for the better.

Unfortunately, those who seek to distract themselves from productive work also tend to distract others from productive work. The unproductive person is setting up an alibi to explain or justify low productivity. The fact that others are recruited into his or her scheme is part of the rationalizing or justification process.

Planning failure

I had a salesperson working for me once who had a cynical, sarcastic sense of humor that amused no one in the office but him. He was a *bubble-popper.* He lived to burst other people's balloons. The time and energy he wasn't spending on his own success, he eagerly spent on spoiling the success of others. His exploits were intended to take the focus off of his own marginal performance.

Turning around this person's attitude was no easy task. After all of my conventional coaching had failed to make a dent in his attitude, I finally asked him to make a written list of everything that didn't work in our business. "Do you mean make a list of all the ways to not make money here?" He asked. I nodded my head. "Well I can do that," he continued confidently, "I do that every day."

I proceeded to wipe the smile off his face by asking him, in light of his last comment, what he had planned for the next day. The light bulb went on above his head. He looked me straight in the eye and, in a more serious tone, said, "My God, I've never stopped to think about that." He suddenly realized that he makes a plan every day to not succeed.

In how many aspects of your life do you make a plan to not succeed? How much energy do you spend every day executing such plans? You don't have to have an irritatingly bad attitude to fall victim to this elaborate procrastination scheme. The idea that people who aren't very visible don't get shot at very much encourages us to lay low.

What better way to lay low than to make sure we never rise very far on the wings of success? Planning for failure is surprisingly more common than you might think. The more comfortable folks become with complacency, the more likely they will operate not in the absence of a plan, but with an actual plan to repeat the things that are known to fail.

The cynical man who worked for me turned his thinking around 180 degrees and his personal performance broke out of its slump. He resolved to discontinue repeating what he knew didn't work. It is easier said than done. But just acknowledging the existence of such a practice is unsettling enough to keep you on your toes. Refusing to repeat failures takes courage because it elevates the very expectations you've been trying to avoid.

I believe that most people want to be productive. Put another way, I believe most people want the rewards of productivity without the risks. Once the rewards seem more attainable and the risks are exposed as essentially inconsequential, productivity will naturally increase. My salesperson realized that he was causing his own misery, which he gladly exchanged for the possible misery of increasing his personal performance.

He found out that there was no misery in increasing his personal performance. Instead, there was a great deal of support and encouragement from those around him, which pleased him to no end. When you give up your plan for failure and replace it with a plan to increase personal performance, the payoff far exceeds the misery of occupying yourself with unimportant matters.

Many people who repeat what they know doesn't work do so in only certain aspects of their lives and work. You don't have to be a complete delinquent to be guilty of petty distraction. It's possible to have success in a variety of ways and to also sabotage your complete victory by holding back certain key components that are needed to bring everything to completion.

I've seen countless people make incredible strides to increase personal performance only to stumble just short of the finish line. Every time, I'm surprised and scratch my head. I just want to believe that, once someone gets past the first few major roadblocks to higher productivity, s/he will overcome every obstacle, internal or external.

If every one of us took the time to honestly evaluate our work on a daily basis, no doubt we would turn up a number of things that are productivity-blocking, repeated failures. When a plan has been established for increasing productivity, it's easier to flag nonproductive behavior. All you have to do is hold up your daily activities against the backdrop of the plan and evaluate which tasks and activities did not promote progress.

Goals vs. fantasies

In effective planning, it's important to know the difference between what is a legitimate goal and what's not. A fantasy is not a goal. By definition a fantasy is imagination unrestrained by reality. A goal is a fantasy with a concrete, measurable, realizable plan for achievement. If you don't know specifically what you have to do to on a daily basis, in addition to your customary activities, you don't have a real goal.

It's the combination of desired rewards and a plan to achieve them that make a goal worth your energy and attention. Some public speakers make a lot of money by getting up m front of audiences flailing their arms and jumping up and down until the audience is doing the same thing. They do it in the name of *enthusiasm.* These motivational speakers do in fact inspire enthusiasm in their audiences—for the moment.

A purely motivational presentation without redeeming substance will wear off by the time most people get to the cars in the parking lot and certainly by the time the audience wakes up the next morning. As I discussed earlier, each of us faces a moment of truth each and every day. Our inspired enthusiasm comes from rededicating ourselves to the *high-performance process* that brings more of our unique strengths to the surface.

As long as an intended goal remains a fantasy, excitement and enthusiasm will turn into frustration and disappointment. Hanging a picture of the expensive car, sailboat, dream house, secluded beach, or other material goal on your refrigerator or office wall—without a concrete plan for achievement—will ultimately produce resentment when you discover that you're not getting any closer to living your fantasy.

Looking at a picture is not the same thing as taking action to identify and do those things that you know will bring reality closer to imagination. I've seen people in companies across America who have pictures of all sorts of things on their office walls. Sadly, the pictures are often old and yellowed with age because they've hung there so long.

One fellow had a picture of a Rolls Royce above his desk. It was so old. The edges were cracked, taped together and cracked again. I asked that man about the picture and he confirmed that it was his goal to own a Rolls Royce. I asked how long he had been pursuing that goal and he confirmed that it had been a long time, many years in fact.

I next asked the man what he was doing over and above his regular daily activities to get his hands on a Rolls Royce. He was stumped. He went on to tell me that all he was told to do was hang the picture up where he could see it every day and one day he would find it in his driveway. Even though his life experience confirmed it, he was surprised to hear me say that simply doing what he ordinarily does wouldn't get him any more than he already had.

Breathtaking moments

Mary Lawrence (the woman who nearly lost her life in an automobile accident and went on to be a record-breaking real estate salesperson) hung her pink dress in fhe closet where she would see it every day. Mary knew exactly what she needed to do on a daily basis to make that dream come true. In a personal moment of truth, she stood at her own crossroads each day and made a decision. The realization of her goal was the net result of the decisions she made day after day. She was visually reminded of her goal each day, but she also had a plan in place to guide her actions toward the meeting of imagination and reality in her life. She executed her plan.

When I presented her with the trophy for being the number-one salesperson, the award she had predicted winning a year before, I was reminded of an expression I had once heard. After Mary had glided toward the podium to accept the award amidst a standing ovation, I told the audience that we shouldn't measure life by how many breaths we take, but by how many breathtaking moments we experience. The number of breathtaking moments we experience is directly proportional to the amount of effort we invest in our plans for achievement.

Time divisions for better planning

Just as goals are subdivided into three categories, *financial, lifestyle* and *personal growth,* so, too, is planning divided into three categories for the purpose of identifying length of execution. The three categories are:

1. Short-term (up to one year).
2. Medium-term (one to five years).
3. Long-term (more than five years).

The length of time you allow yourself to realize a goal should be determined by a realistic timetable more than on the intensity of your desire to reach the goal. A young couple without any savings might *want* to buy an expensive house in one year, but it's not realistic. Without any financial assistance, their goal might be better served by setting up some intermediate steps such as saving the money for a down payment on a more affordable home in 12 months and then moving up to a more expensive home in five years or so.

Remember that a goal needs to be attainable. If a plan is not given sufficient time to be properly executed, it's doomed. Plans of any length need to be thought of in daily increments. If adding up the daily efforts puts you somewhere between one and five years, you've got yourself a medium-term goal.

Don't fall into the trap of thinking that you can simply double or triple your daily effort and speed up the realization of your goal. It might simply be unrealistic to expect so much of yourself. Nobody is superhuman. Everyone has required regular tasks to do in order to provide food, clothing and shelter for the household. How much additional effort can you and will you put forth each day to attain your goal?

Goals that relate to home purchases, home improvements, education, career and family all need to be planned in reference to the length of time needed to properly accomplish the required tasks. Logging daily efforts toward goal attainment requires dedicated discipline. Keeping the big picture in perspective requires vision. Dedication, discipline and vision must all work harmoniously if you expect successful goal attainment.

Small bites

The good news about breaking down goals into daily efforts is that the efforts you face each day are far less overwhelming than the overall process. When I think about writing a book, I see images of that enormous, 300-page manuscript sitting on my desk. It's intimidating. But when I chart a goal of 10 to 15 pages per day, suddenly the task is reasonable. When the enormity of an entire project starts to make your knees weak; immediately focus on your much more manageable daily tasks.

Small bites are never as intimidating as the thought of swallowing something whole. Use caution. Just because you've broken down your plan into small, digestible portions, don't take the daily tasks so lightly that you begin to slack off. When writing a book, I can imagine how easy it would be to skip a day here and a day there until I'm faced with writing 50 pages per day to keep pace with my deadline.

Looking at 50 pages instead of my usual 10 to 15 is a great reminder that "a stitch in time saves nine." To help emphasize the importance of keeping pace with your plan, you should celebrate the accomplishment of each day's tasks. I don't celebrate the writing of 15 pages the same way that I celebrate the book after it's completed.

However, I do acknowledge my daily accomplishment by writing the new page count on a post-it note and sticking it to the edge of the computer screen. When you're working on a project with a specified time allocation for completion, you often get into a "zone" when the daily extra effort comes automatically. That can be a trap too. But over time, dedication to daily tasks actually forms a positive habit and the progress seems to accelerate.

The planning process

You need to *write each goal down*. Holding your dreams in your head doesn't count. Writing down the goal gives it greater focus and commitment. Included in the first draft of your goal must be the time division I just discussed. How long do you predict it will take to reach your goal—short-term, medium-term or long-term? Listing your goals on paper, including estimated time of execution, focuses your thinking on the tasks required for goal attainment rather than on the intimidating big picture. It's okay to post a picture of your desired reward as long as your written goal and its timetable are posted right next to it.

Next, *establish a timetable* by breaking down the short-term, medium-term or long-term time division into daily increments. If the daily steps seem too large and unreasonable, you need to move into a longer overall time division. You can always add more time to goal attainment if you fall short of your mark. Just remember that every time you fall short, you build disappointment and make it harder on yourself the next time. So be as realistic as possible the first time.

Concentrate on results. From the outset, achievement of the daily goals must be considered part of the overall mission. You're doing whatever it is you're doing for a reason. You want something. That's why you set out in the first place. Your efforts should produce the type of enthusiasm that you felt when you committed to the goal in the first place.

Be aware that the desired outcome can become too consuming and obliterate the daily tasks required. Results in daily terms and in longer time division terms go hand in hand. At the planning stage, you need to include some method of monitoring progress.

Get started and stick with it. Winston Churchill said, "Never, never, never give up." Unless there is some material change in your desired rewards, there's probably no reason to stop other than fatigue or fear of success. Neither fatigue nor fear of success is acceptable outcomes to your goal-achievement process.

High-performance people know that they need to plan for the temptation to quit. It's going to come. Even though you start with all the conviction of Winston Churchill, you might turn into W.C. Fields without realizing it. W.C. Fields said, "If at first you don't succeed, try again. Then quit, there's no use being a damn fool about it." When the inevitable temptation to quit arrives, back off at your own peril. Do you want others to see you as Churchill or W.C. Fields?

Celebrate the achievement of a goal and immediately replace it with a new goal. As mentioned, appropriate celebrations along the way are merely a prelude to the bit party you should throw when the overriding goal is achieved. All celebrations are important when kept in context. But intermediary celebrations need to include a look ahead to what's left and major celebrations must be the launching pads for bigger and better things to come.

Don't miss your own victory party by immediately diving into a new major task. Instead, acknowledge that what's just been accomplished can and will be followed by equal or greater accomplishments. The establishment of a new goal should be part of the vision, complete celebration. As soon as it's practical draft a new with a plan for accomplishment.

Establishment of a new goal is critical to your ongoing success because you will feel an inevitable letdown following the accomplishment of the previous goal. That's why we suffer from the "post-holiday blues/blahs/depression." Without something to look forward to, there isn't much to be excited about. When there's not much to be excited about, nothing seems very exciting.

In goal achievement, like in any much-anticipated event or celebration, the buildup and anticipation is most of the fun. That's why a realistic, manageable timetable is critical. You need to feel that the accomplishment is possible. Holidays come every year. They're on the calendar. The achievement of your goals should be as dependable.

In developing your plan, account for the post-accomplishment letdown by planning for the establishment of a new goal. You know how your emotional calendar works, so plan accordingly. I did a program in Hawaii shortly after the New Year. I asked the audience, who had come from the mainland for the conference, if they ever felt post-holiday depression. Virtually every hand went up.

I asked how many of them had experienced their usual post-holiday letdown after Christmas a few weeks earlier. No hands went up. Why? All of them were anticipating their trip to Hawaii in early January. Their much-anticipated celebration of Christmas and New Years was immediately followed by the anticipation of a new celebration.

I remember having new-car fever in the worst way. When I bought my Porsche, I got over it. For the first few weeks after the purchase, I used to get up in the middle of the night and go down to the garage and look at it. Standing there in my pajamas, admiring my car, the celebration continued. Now, I sleep through the night and find the car waiting for me in the morning. I still love it, but the anticipation has evaporated.

Some of the NASA astronauts who went to the moon suffered terrible post-mission depression after they returned. When you work so hard, for so long on achieving a goal like going to the moon, how do you follow that? You and I can always say that, when we've done everything there is to do on this planet, we still have the moon to look forward to.

Finally, *evaluate your progress each year on your birthday.* Birthdays are intensely personal mile markers on life's journey. Regardless of how many goals you've planned in whatever time divisions, your birthday is a great opportunity to check progress. I challenge you to write yourself a letter, seal it in an envelope and open it on your next birthday.

In the letter, tell yourself what you plan to have accomplished by that time. If just thinking about writing that letter is making you sweat, you're normal. A letter to yourself with a commitment to accomplish certain things proves the power of writing down goals. Documented goals can't be ignored with good conscience. Courage is one of the personal characteristics I listed for high-performance people. You'll need courage to write that letter every year. Keeping your promises to yourself might be a feeling you've rarely felt before.

Recapping the planning process:

1. Make a written list of your goals, including time divisions.

2. Break down the timetable into manageable tasks and deadlines.
3. Concentrate on results.
4. Get started and stick with it.
5. Celebrate when a goal is achieved and simultaneously replace it with a new goal.
6. Evaluate your progress each year on your birthday.

Making it happen: 6 thoughts

"I don't mind taking chances, but I never leave anything to chance."
—Charles Lindbergh

Lindbergh's comment does not contradict itself. The *high-performance process* requires you to step out of your comfort zone and experience new things. Because venturing into uncharted territory is uncomfortable, you're bound to feel anxious and hesitant. As Lindbergh lifted off on his solo flight across the Atlantic Ocean he must have felt every bit as anxious as you and I will ever feel.

The best way to minimize anxiety when boldly taking your life to another level is to do your homework. Be prepared. Expecting the unexpected makes the unexpected less of an unsettling surprise when it occurs. Chance is unavoidable when you endeavor to push back your horizons. However, preparation reduces the risk.

Lindbergh's point is to be a *smart* adventurer. Life without adventure is a boring existence. Your commitment to becoming a high-performance person will bring you as much adventure as you can handle. Like Lindbergh, your journey will be more productive and lastingly beneficial when you bring knowledge and skill to the process, leaving as little to chance as possible.

Lindbergh's solo flight across the Atlantic was measured in hours. Preparation for the flight took *years*. Whether you're aware of it or not, your life to this point has been preparation for the decisions you're about to make. The planning phase of the *high-performance process* is the formal, structured processing of what you have learned and experienced.

Thought one: Organization

Organization means different things to different people. What it must mean to you is the ability to look at your resources as they relate to your stated goals. Whatever you have learned and experienced needs to be inventoried as it relates to your intention to become a high-performance person. As I've mentioned, you are a storehouse of valuable talents, information and experience.

Continuing the idea that Elbert Hubbard set forth about organizing your energies around a goal, your stated objectives become the focal point of all that you've accumulated in your storehouse. That's organization. Merely keeping copious notes and well-documented files on all manner of information doesn't necessarily identify the ultimate purpose that the well-organized information serves.

Thought two: Planning

Proper prior planning positively prevents poor performances.

Back home in the coal-mining country of Southern Illinois they used to say it like this, "It's okay to have a tiger by the tail—if you know what to do next!" I learned this lesson flying supersonic fighters in air shows. When I was flying 25 feet above the concrete runway at 700 miles per hour, it was a thrill to watch people, trees, and buildings shoot past my wing tips.

After I swung out into a big teardrop-shaped turn and came back past the crowd, I was flying 100 miles-per-hour slower, *upside-down.* The concrete runway flashed by 25 feet below my canopy at 600 miles-per-hour. One word I never wanted to hear myself utter during an air show was "Oops." Flying as close to the edge as I did, that would have been the last word I would have uttered.

It was countless hours of training and preparation that taught me to climb before I made my teardrop-shaped turn. Striking a wing tip while rolling into a 700 mile-per-hour turn at 25 feet would have produced a 700 mile-per-hour cartwheel. The crowd might have loved it and I probably would have made the evening news, but it would have been my first and final performance.

Likewise, it was exhaustive preparation that helped me to remember, while flying upside-down, hanging from my straps, that my controls were *reversed*. Had I lapsed for a moment and pulled back on the stick to climb out, I would have buried my nose in the pavement at 600 miles-per-hour without time to note my error and correct it.

The unexpected will come, but it will be expected. I mean that to be a contradiction. Proper planning will bring you through the predictable, leaving you the flexibility to deal with the unexpected—precisely because you anticipated the unexpected. When you're unprepared, anything that comes along can derail you. When you're prepared, it takes a catastrophe to knock you off balance. And even then preparation accelerates recovery.

Thought three: Less time and more action

There's a term in the business world that I hear with increasing regularity. It's called *sprinting*. Apparently business people are beginning to realize that there is a natural human tendency to make a job last as long as it's given time to be accomplished. As a result, many people take eight hours to do what could be done in four. But, if four hours of work is all that's required of them in an eight-hour day, the four-hour job would take eight.

Clearly, I'm not describing high-performance people. Yet, all of us tend to drag things out if we're not paying attention. To concentrate action and get a job done in the optimum amount of time gives the opportunity to relax and reflect a bit before charging into your next event. People who appear calm and organized around the office are the people who know how to get things done efficiently and swiftly.

The people who look as if they're on the brink of disaster at all times are probably the ones who take too long to get started on tasks, take too long to accomplish them, and are therefore in a constant state of catch-up. The person who chooses to focus energy around goals and concentrate action for rapid results is far more likely to lead a low-stress life than someone who is always behind.

Poor planning and inefficient use of time lead to disorganization and frustration. Proper planning and emphasis on action lead to a richer existence. The net result of proper planning is to add more life to your years, not more years to your life. Being finished with an important task feels good. Being buried in work with no relief in sight feels hopeless.

Thought four: Change the present and change the future

You have no control over the past. You have no control over the future. You only have control over the present. People hear me say that and disagree saying, "But, Danny, isn't everything we do supposed to control the future?" Unfortunately, we have no control over whether there even *is* a future. That possibility is in the hands of a power much bigger than we are.

Realistically, all we can do in the present is to set the stage for what happens in the future. However, not taking charge of our lives in the *now* cuts our future adrift. Just bobbing in the waves now, without any attempt to power or steer your ship, means that you'll still be drifting aimlessly tomorrow, no matter what the future brings.

What you establish today by concentrating your energies around a goal makes tomorrow a better-defined opportunity, even though you won't be able to influence tomorrow until it arrives. By planning and committing yourself to the *high-performance process* now, your course is charted and the resources are made ready for the decisions you make while standing at tomorrow's crossroads.

The fellow with the picture of the Rolls Royce on his office wall wasn't actively engaged in any organized effort to do the things today that would influence his future. Somehow he thought that by merely picturing a future the way he would like it to be, he was going to exert some cosmic energy to create future change. He, like the rest of us, only has the *now* to work with.

As I pointed out to him, the change he needed to be concerned with should have been in the present, not the future. It's what you do today and every day that determines, to the greatest possible degree, the quality of your future. It might be exciting to dream and fantasize about the future and all of the potential it holds, but it's a lot *more* exciting to realize that you can plant seeds today that will bloom tomorrow.

Thought five: Time to be creative, relax, and live

One way that working intelligently and effectively in the present will improve the quality of your future is by clearing away worries and responsibilities that would otherwise be carried forward and added to your future burdens. Creativity, an essential element of the *high-performance process,* requires some space.

Although the future is not under your control, you can do yourself a favor by dispensing with as much clutter as possible now to be ready when the time and opportunity arises for creative thought. I'm referring to the reflective, stream-of-consciousness type of creative thinking, not the creative outlook that you should bring to everything you do.

Rest and relaxation are important to recharging your batteries. All work and no play, over time, makes you an increasingly unproductive individual. Some people feel too guilty to relax. Don't confuse emotionally driven workaholism with high performance. Bringing more of yourself to the work you do makes the work more satisfying and fulfilling. Bringing more of your uniqueness to your play strikes a better balance between work and relaxation.

In total, the quality of your life is determined by how much of your unique identity is reflected in your work, play, and lifestyle. Good planning is critical to keeping these things in proper balance and perspective. The *high-performance process* is a method of encouraging cross-pollination between the various aspects of your life. By bringing the elements into balance and harmony, the whole becomes a more fertile environment for doing what makes you happiest.

Thought six: Live life, don't portray it

Somerset Maugham said that. Maugham's imperative brings the planning of time and resources into alignment with the basic theme of the *high-performance process.* That is the understanding that your talents, knowledge, and experience combine to form a truly unique creature. The closer you get to living in a way that reflects your uniqueness, the more your productivity increases.

Proper planning of your time and resources is the antidote for stress. When you're trying to portray an image that someone else thinks you should portray, you're not functioning in your strongest state. That's not good for you and that's not good for the people who rely on you. The greatest stress you can encounter is to attempt conforming to an image that you're not prepared or equipped to handle.

Planning is the focusing of your energies around a goal, not someone else's energy. To have maximum control over your life, that is in terms of your personal talents, knowledge, and experience, you must develop a strategy that reflects what you bring to the situation. When that's accomplished, you're living your life and not play-acting in a miscast role. Living life on your terms means maximizing your personal performance potential, which is the lowest-stress environment.

Reasons people don't plan their time

We've all done it: caught ourselves unprepared and overwhelmed with work or other obligations that could have been easily managed with a little planning. It's in those moments that we berate ourselves and wonder why we don't do what we know we should do—plan the use of our time. It doesn't matter whether we ask ourselves or if someone else asks us, the perfect answers always seem to come out of the same script.

Each of the common answers that follow are undefendable in light of what we already know about the *high-performance process.* Nevertheless, such excuses pop out of our mouths from time to time, given sufficient frustration. Once you've enrolled yourself in the *high-performance process,* at least you can dismiss such foolishness as soon as it appears.

For example, one of the most common excuses for not planning time better is, "It would limit my freedom." High-performance people know that proper planning increases personal freedom. Greater control over the positive and negative aspects of your day-to-day activities result in maximizing what you want and minimizing what you don't want.

Those with the most freedom are those with effective control over their lives. Those with effective control over their lives are high performers who understand the process of planning and executing the tasks and activities that fill the day. Lack of planning makes you a victim of other people's agendas. With proper planning, *you* set more of your own agenda. That sounds like freedom to me.

Another excuse offered for not planning is, "Things are just too unpredictable." The statement that things are unpredictable is basically true. The implied futility of planning isn't. While it's true that we can't predict the future and things can and will happen that are beyond our control, it still doesn't make sense to abandon the very thing that offers us hope.

Why should athletes practice for the big game if they can't predict exactly what's going to happen? Why do pilots and astronauts prepare so meticulously for their missions if they might encounter the unpredictable?

Why do financial institutions make such a big deal about investing for retirement? You never know what might happen between now and then. Even though time can't be socked away in an individual retirement account or in a coffee can buried in the backyard, the disciplined habits you acquire today insure that whatever you encounter in the future won't be as threatening or potentially devastating as it would be for an unprepared person.

Saying that an unpredictable future makes planning moot is like saying that doctors shouldn't bother studying so hard in medical school. Would you look up from the operating table and say, "I don't blame you for skipping most of your medical classes, Doc. When you get into these surgery situations, who knows what's going to happen?"

I think you would prefer that the surgeon with the scalpel be as well prepared as possible with substantial thought invested in the surgical strategy. Aren't you operating on your life every day? Shouldn't you invest in your future by giving ample thought to planning your personal surgical strategy? It's precisely because the future is unpredictable that you're better off being prepared.

How about this one: "I just don't have time to plan my time." Somebody switch on a light. Time is the critical commodity here. Trying to save time by not planning how your time is going to be best used makes no sense. All you're doing by ignoring time planning is guaranteeing that most of your time will be used very inefficiently.

You already know the frustrating liabilities of being on someone else's schedule. Yet that's exactly what you do if you don't chart your path in advance. Sure, unpredictable obstacles will leap into your path. Others will make demands on your time. However, these distractions and disruptions are far more manageable when you've thought ahead and prepared your own agenda, complete with the flexible anticipation of interruptions.

At the bottom line, high-performance people know that proper planning *increases freedom, makes life more predictable* and *clears more time* to be used at your personal discretion. The use of excuses usually means that someone is not yet comfortable with moving their life to the next performance level. By evading increased productivity with excuses, they're giving tacit confirmation that planning *does* make a difference.

Don't try to convince Mary Lawrence that she would sacrifice her freedom, that the economy, the customers, and the market are too unpredictable, or that she is wasting valuable time when she plans her strategy for success. She's living proof that planning pays off. You can't tell me that intricate planning and preparation didn't save my life a thousand times, both figuratively and literally, during my years as a supersonic fighter pilot and a business executive.

Don't claim that you don't have enough information to plan with. All anybody can do is plan with the information they've got. If it's fear that's driving your unwillingness to predict the future, you need to remember the admonition of the actor, Glenn Ford, that either you or fear will be in charge. You know that planning will make demands on your performance. If that's a frightening thought, find out why.

Controlling your time: 3 steps

You might be among the people who have all the best intentions about increasing your personal productivity but feel as if time is your worst enemy. Other than the fact that you've probably adopted some of the time-wasting habits I just outlined, you no doubt feel as if time controls you and not the other way around. High-performance people know and accept that they can't alter the passing of time. Instead, they sharpen their skills at managing their time allotment. Proper planning and management of your available time will provide you with the maximum control possible. Peter Drucker says it takes three steps to manage time.

Time management step 1: Record your time

Most people claim they're aware of how they spend their time. Almost without exception, they're wrong. Your memory is a horrible liar when it comes to accounting for your time. You would think that keeping track of time is somehow related to keeping track of calories on a diet. It never ceases to amaze me how I can keep gaining weight when I'm sure my caloric intake is going down. At least as far as my memory serves I'm eating less.

Even though time seems like an elusive commodity and you're always a day late, your memory will probably still tell you that you're putting every available second to the best use possible. To get an accurate picture of how conscious you really are when it comes to time, keep a log of how you spend your waking hours. I guarantee that you'll be surprised.

It's physically easy to do. The avoidant part of you will procrastinate. Once you break through your procrastination, simply sit down with your daily planner at the end of each day, for three days, and record how your time was spent. Be specific. If a one-hour block has a meeting noted, think back to whether the meeting actually took place.

You might have only spent part of that hour in a meeting. How was the rest of the hour spent? Traveling to and from the meeting? Talking to someone on the telephone or coffee machine? Were the conversations personal or business-related? You can immediately see that three days spent accounting for your time, morning, noon, and night, will bring you face to face with the realities of your personal productivity. I predict you'll appreciate the urgent need for time management—*now!*

Time management step 2: Manage your time

"Until we can manage time, we can manage nothing else."
—Peter F. Drucker

You can't manage time itself in the sense of speeding it up, slowing it down, or otherwise altering it. Time is like the ocean. We're all in the same sea and nobody can realistically change the volume of water. The only decision left is whether to sink or swim in it. There is more to come shortly on the specifics of time management. For now, just etch into the inside of your forehead that managing time means swimming in it and not sinking in it.

Time management step 3: Consolidate your time

As a prelude to a full-scale organizational effort, it's important to begin looking for tasks and chores that can be grouped together in more efficient units. A phrase I like to use is, "Don't just plan your time, time your plan." In other words, you can very deliberately schedule time for even the most minuscule task without considering how the grouping of specific tasks can add a great deal to the time efficiency of your day.

You can group chores together because they are geographically compatible, because they call for similar tools, because they call for the same mode of thinking and operating, or for any other reason that eliminates an unnecessary duplication of effort. Your goal in grouping tasks together is to avoid covering the same ground more often than is absolutely necessary.

Reevaluating your time for increased earnings

Perhaps more than anyone else, salespeople understand and appreciate the direct link between time and money. If a salesperson is working on a commission basis, any time not spent in the pursuit of a sale is nonproductive time. In the business world the same is true of everybody. It's just harder to see. Everybody in a for-profit or not-for-profit enterprise is there to ultimately serve a customer.

Sometimes customers are internal to the organization in the form of co-workers. At other times the customer is someone outside of the organization who wants and/or needs the product or service that the organization exists to provide. Most of the time, people serve both internal and external customers. As such, everyone's time is tied to the quality of service and performance of the organization as a whole.

The example I'm about to use will focus on earnings as they're tied to commissioned sales. However, the analogy holds for every type of vocational or avocational assignment. No matter what you do, the relationship between executing your regular activities and how you use your time is the same. You can break down whatever process you're involved with into time-related components.

First, *decide what you want to earn in a year*. In broader terms, what do you want to accomplish in a year? Using the time division method I described earlier, use a 12-month track that's appropriate and realistic for a short-term goal. Make sure that you're not selling your talents, knowledge, and experience short. The target you choose should reflect what you are capable of and have good reason to expect of yourself.

Second, *divide that goal into 50 weekly goals*. (I'm assuming that you'll allow yourself a two-week vacation.) If the annual goal is an earnings figure, then it's easy to divide that figure by 50. If your goal is subject to seasonal influences, take that into account as you break down the larger goal into its more attainable and digestible smaller parts.

Third, *divide your weekly target by the number or hours you work in a week*. This is where the time-planning process rubber meets the road. How many hours are you willing and able to work week-in and week-out to reach your goal? Most people stumble here because they bite off more than they can chew in a day. Planning to work on your goal eight hours a day, six days a week, might seem doable when you're drafting your plan, but it's not. Trust me.

Someone once told me that it's impossible to lead a successful life. It's only possible to lead a successful *day*. If you already completed the exercise of logging how efficiently you use your daily time allotment, you already know that a day is filled with distractions, disruptions, and altered plans. You must account for how much of your day you can realistically expect to devote to accomplishing your plan.

Fourth, *divide your hourly projection by four.* Now you have a 15-minute segment of one year's worth of effort. Now you can ask yourself throughout the day, "What was my last 15 minutes worth?" Time is rushing past you nonstop. The only time you can work with it is in the moment that it passes through you. At that moment, your future becomes your past. The value of your past, relative to your future, is determined in the *now.*

For example, if you want to earn $100,000 in the next 12 months, that's $2,000 per week. Divide $2,000 per week by 40 hours, to get $50. Then, $50 per hour divided into 15-minute segments is $12.50. Is every 15-minute segment of your workday worth $12.50?

If your 15-minute segments are not being used efficiently enough to bring in $12.50, then the $100,000 annual figure is unrealistic. Rather than give up on the annual figure, wouldn't it make more sense to increase your performance in the 15-minute segments of your day? Get into the habit of evaluating your productivity in 15-minute intervals.

What was the value of my last 15 minutes? That question should be tattooed on the back of your hand. It should be displayed on the back of the nameplate on your desk. It should be labeled on the cradle of the biggest time-waster of them all, your telephone. It's important to be as conscious of your time as possible.

Don't waste your time worrying about larger time increments. You have no control over the larger time segments except for what you're doing in the present moment. By focusing on the efficient and effective use of the present moment, you are establishing the value and quality of your future. There will always be the unexpected to contend with, but you're filling in as much of the painting as you can— the way you want it to look when you get there.

Once you're aware of how your time is spent throughout the day, you'll be able to write yourself a mental check at the end of each day for what you feel the day was worth. Did you exchange each hour of your time that day for $25? Was it less? Was it more? Don't be lulled into complacency by a big day. Unusually productive days are something to feel good about, but they can tempt you to slack off as well.

Checking up on your productivity every 15 minutes doesn't mean you shouldn't take breaks and stop for lunch. Rest and relaxation are important to your ongoing productivity. The high-performance person appreciates how recharging his or her batteries affects overall performance. Being vigilant about how effectively your time is being used provides helpful insight into how valuable the time is that you spend resting, having lunch and/or conversing with customers and colleagues.

Once, when Thomas Edison was called upon to deliver a message to a graduating class, the prolific American inventor said:

Always be interested in whatever you're doing at the time and think only of that thing in all its bearings and mastery. Don't mind the clock, but keep at it and let nature indicate the necessity of rest. After resting, go after the work again with the same interest. The world pays big prices for [those] who know the values and satisfactions of persistent hard work.

Identify time-wasters

There are certain criteria that you can use as a template or time-waste screening device. There will always be occasions when you won't know that time and effort have been wasted until it's too late. But in most cases you can screen out time-wasters in advance, if you know what to look for. Your 15-minute productivity reviews will show much better results if you scrape some of these time-wasting barnacles off the hull of your ship.

1. Doing something with no return.
2. Doing something that keeps you from a higher priority task.
3. Attempting too much at once.
4. Poor time scheduling.
5. Procrastination.
6. Not listening.
7. Not saying no.
8. Doing instead of delegating.
9. Personal disorganization.

10. Snap decisions.
11. Inefficient telephone use.
12. Imitating the way an inefficient person carries out his or her day.

When I was a salesperson, just out of the Air Force, I had a boss who would come by my desk and ask, "What are you doing there, Danny?" Depending on how I answered him, he would usually follow with the question, "How is that putting money in your pocket—right now?" If I had to admit that what I was doing wasn't putting money in my pocket at the moment, he would keep after me.

"How is what you're doing now going to put money into your pocket a month from now, or three months from now?" I caught his drift pretty quickly and changed the way I thought about using my time. There are quite a few things that are fun to do, but bring no return. I'm not suggesting that you shouldn't have fun. Just put it in perspective regarding the value of your time.

Favorite activities will usually wind up as misplaced priorities. Will a close examination of your recent history reveal that you spend a disproportionate amount of time on personal rather than professional activities? Fortunately for you, the *high-performance process* brings personal and professional interests into alignment.

It's also important to realistically assess your activities in light of your documented priorities. All too often, we go for the easiest thing to do at the moments, figuring that we'll shoot all the slow rabbits first and then have time for the more important tasks. Somehow it never works out that way. That's why prioritizing is so critical.

Never dive into your list at number two, three, four, or below. Never be caught working on your number-two, three, or four priority while the big number one is still sitting up there at the top of the list. When the number-one item is dispatched, then number two becomes the new number one. That way, you're never making a second- or third-priority effort. You'll always be working on your top priority.

Attempting too much at once is a sure way to waste time. More than that, adding one too many things to your plate means you'll probably do an inferior job on everything. If your eyes are bigger than your ability, you're setting yourself up to be chump instead of the hero. Not only will you do a poor job, you'll probably dam up your own progress and the efficiency of the organization by having to go back and cover the same ground all over again.

As I've just detailed, poor time scheduling will rob you of your opportunity to excel. The breakdown of your time allotment into daily, hourly and 15-minute segments keeps the value of your time in the front of your mind and makes poor or inefficient time planning a repugnant thought. Once you're aware of how valuable your time is, I doubt that you will give a low priority in your planning process.

Procrastination rears its ugly head once again on this list of time wasters because it's so common. Procrastination is a subtle enemy that sneaks up on you in a variety of insidious ways. You won't usually realize that you're procrastinating until you do your 15-minute check up and/or check to see if in fact you're busily working on priority number one.

Not listening is an incredibly obnoxious time waster. When I was an executive, I adopted the policy that I only explained things once. That might sound cruel and unusual, but it was a matter of survival. Too many people would be told what the plan was only to come back and waste their time and my time asking me to tell them all over again. As soon as I started allowing them to twist in the wind if they didn't get it the first time, my staffs hearing and retention made a remarkable improvement.

Because of the inevitable relational dynamics that exist in the workplace, it's highly probable that somebody is going to foist some work off on you that they should rightfully be doing. You must be able to say no. This doesn't mean that you cease being a team player and barricade yourself in your office. High-performance people know how essential it is to draw appropriate responsibility boundaries with others in the organization. Invariably, the most respected workers are those who have a helpful spirit, but do not allow themselves to be exploited.

Your ability to delegate comes with rank and skill. You must have the right to delegate, based upon your standing in the organization.

But more than that, you must have the planning and people skills to spread the workload fairly. Doing things that someone else in the group is better-suited for or can do with less drain on the organization's resources is selfish at best and ultimately unfair to everyone in the company.

Personal disorganization that results from your refusal to properly plan your time and resources will kill any hope you might have of using your time effectively. If your plan is to remain as ineffective as possible, staying personally disorganized is a sure way to do it. What many people don't understand is that their personal organizational habits have a profound impact on the effectiveness of the organization as a whole.

Making snap decisions without properly thinking through the benefits and potential liabilities will come back to haunt you in the form of time wasted undoing your work. Once in awhile you might get lucky and score with a seat-of-the-pants call, but I wouldn't bet the farm on it—if you want to keep the farm.

Folklore might be filled with the heroics of risk-takers, but nobody I know wants to fly with a seat-of-the-pants pilot. I'd rather fly with Charles Lindbergh who leaves nothing to chance. When you think about it, just working through the *high-performance process* itself will provide all the challenge a sane person needs.

The telephone can murder your time. I always recommend that, if your phone system doesn't display how long a call has been in progress, you jot down the time that a phone call starts, whether you placed it or it was incoming. It's too easy to chat away valuable time and think that you're accomplishing something. Chatting on the telephone is a favorite distraction for most people who find it entertaining.

Use the telephone wisely. When the phone rings or when you place a call, don't look at the upcoming conversation as an opportunity to get in touch with the world that you've sealed yourself off from. The more you have your nose buried in solitary work, the more likely you'll seize the opportunity to make your telephone conversations social contacts that fill your need to interact with someone. Instead, plan to meet your interaction requirements during your breaks or lunch hour. Use the telephone as a business tool.

The grass is always greener on the other side of the fence. It's not unusual to see someone who seems to be having more fun with what they're doing than you are. Of course, once you've brought as much of your unique talents, knowledge, and experience to the job as possible through the *high-performance process,* imitating the low performers' behavior will cease to be a temptation.

Suffice to say that you might, at times, be tempted to imitate someone who has a less responsible, more casual attitude (and performance) about them and gives the *appearance* of enjoying himself or herself more than you do. The way that you increase the level of satisfaction you feel is to be more like *you,* not more like somebody else.

Getting organized

Using your documented goals as the spine, build an organizational skeleton. Organizing your talents, knowledge and experience around a goal means that the goal must remain central to your organizational efforts. You can do all of the things I'm about to suggest without having a purpose beyond putting things around you in order.

You can have a well-ordered life without having accomplishing anything. The commonly uttered phrase, "I've got to get organized" is a bit misleading. The thought that merely getting organized will put your life back on track is a myth. You can have the most elaborate filing and time-accountability system in the world and still go nowhere.

From time to time, I've found myself organizing my heart out only to discover that I'm really procrastinating. One of the most popular methods to avoid tackling truly important tasks is to straighten up around the home or office. It seems like the more imposing the assignment, the more important it is to have all of your pencils sharpened, all of your paper clips sorted by size and color, and the desk must be dusted.

Before you get started, you'll want to answer that mail that's been sitting there for six months and you haven't even begun to clean out your drawers. There are people who have spotless offices where everything in the world is neatly filed alphabetically, chronologically and geographically. When you ask them what they do with all their data, they give you a blank stare. They're ready for anything, they just don't know what it is yet.

Organization is critical to the *high-performance process*. However, any attempt at organization must be anchored to a goal or set of goals if the organization is to be meaningful. Form must follow function. Organize because your continued growth and success depend on it. Organize with a purpose!

Here are some tips:

1. Purchase a daily planner.

I talk to people all the time who claim they plan their time and then take out a tiny pocket calendar to prove it. Not only is it too small to use for detailed time planning, it's usually a month-at-a-glance calendar. With one half-inch square for each day, you could write "pick up laundry" and it would look like you have a big day planned.

A time-planning aid must have each day broken down into the 15-minute segments I described earlier. As you fill in each line, you're not trying to kill time, you're trying to fill time. Each 15-minute segment is important. Each 15-minute segment must be spent on an activity that moves you closer to your stated objective.

There are a variety of good time systems now available on the market including the electronic organizers such as Palm Pilot. Each one has an elaborate planner and provides training in various methods of time efficiency. No matter how sophisticated or expensive your time-planning system is, the bottom line is still how effectively you organize around your documented goals.

2. Organize your physical environment.

Despite what I said a few paragraphs ago about avoiding responsibility by over-organizing, it's still important to be physically organized. If you're dying to clear away clutter, here's your chance. Take an evening, early morning, or weekend to organize your office, briefcase or car (if that's your office).

The goal in ordering your physical environment is to remove obstructions to progress. What good are having tools and resources if you don't have ready access to them? You don't want to plan efficient use of your time only to be thrown off-schedule looking for the items you need to conduct your daily activities.

Be merciless in throwing things away. If you haven't used something in a year, chances are good that the item is not essential to your ongoing activities. Clutter accumulates when you stash something away for that fantasy project, novel, or other low-priority use that has nothing to do with your ongoing activities.

If you must store low-priority items, establish an archive somewhere away from your place of business. If something is to die for, archive it where your grandchildren will find it someday. Otherwise, *throw it away!* Forego sentiment whenever possible and cut off as much ballast as you can.

There are very few articles or other published resources that couldn't be found through your local library if you really needed them. If you're a pack rat with an enormous accumulation of stuff, chances are good that you're not stockpiling resources for a well-focused project, but rather a wide variety of nonrelated materials in case any of it ever interests you enough to pursue someday.

Put the things you use most frequently closest to you, in a top drawer or your briefcase. People often put things they *intend* to use nearby and then have to dig through those items to get to what they really *need* to use. You must be realistic about what you do and how you spend your time to properly organize yourself.

Set up a filing system so that you can find what you need in a hurry. Anything that's important enough to store is important enough to have access to. A filing system simply refers to a systematic storage strategy with a simple, efficient, and easy to understand retrieval capability.

Time-lapse motion picture photography studies have revealed that people spend a great deal of time reaching for files or objects that could have been stored closer at hand. According to Stephanie Winston, business managers can spend upwards of 150 hours per year just looking for things. To get into economy of motion issues is pretty sophisticated, but the point is relevant to anyone who can benefit from a more efficient physical arrangement.

3. Divide your job into parts.

Determine which elements of your job require the most organization and which elements are less important. Don't waste your time on that proverbial paper clip sorting when you could be setting up a tickler file for following up with clients.

Don't base your decision of what to organize on what's the most disorganized. The least organized aspect of your job might not be the most vital aspect of your job. Priorities matter in organizing as much as being organized.

4. Make sure that you set a deadline for your organizing efforts.

Even if you're not using the organization process to procrastinate about other things, it's possible to drag out the process to the point that it's more of a liability than a benefit. Each step of your organizational plan should be ranked by priority.

5. Get started.

The *intent* to organize your life is different than actually *doing* it. Intent has no positive benefits. If organizing your resources, affairs, etc., is going to help you increase your personal productivity, it makes no sense to delay. High-performance people don't think in terms of delaying the start of something beneficial.

Priority lists

One of the things that Stephanie Winston stresses in her great book, *The Organized Executive,* is the importance of having one master "to do" list. Everything that you know you have to do should be on that list. From the most important task you face, to filling the car with gas on the way home, everything should be on that list. Everything from getting a college degree to getting a new pair of shoes should be listed.

Stephanie further suggests that you visit that list each day and pull out the things that need to be accomplished in the next 24 hours. Even so, there will be a disparity between high-priority and low-priority items. Incidentally, getting a number of low-priority tasks accomplished and out of the way can give you a tremendously liberated feeling. It's important to clear away the stubble as it were. Even so, it's the big tasks that receive your primary attention.

The psychological benefit from crossing items off a list is obvious. When an item is completed and crossed off, a burden has been lifted from your shoulders. After crossing a number of items off the list, what remains will show clearly what still needs to be done. In other words, a list even a partially completed list—will give you your current bearings.

Because the *high-performance process* has a time component, working a priority list helps keep you on schedule. You have a sense about the amount of time each task requires for completion.

What remains to be done on your list is also an estimate of your time frame. Working your priority list will require some flexibility. You will have to make decisions along the way to decide which items should be grouped together and in what order should they be executed.

One of the most frustrating feelings I've ever experienced is to know that there's much to be done but not have an inventory in front of me. High-performance people always have their priority list close at hand and use it constantly to ensure the most effective use of their time. The more often you refer to the list, the more information you retain in your head, giving you an ongoing sense of where you are in your plan for the day.

Setting up a priority system

It's possible to be efficient without being effective. Like the person who organizes without a purpose, you can dispatch tasks, large and small, without much consideration for how those tasks are affecting goal accomplishment. Busying yourself with task after task, without regard for how those activities propel you toward the accomplishment of your documented goals, is like rowing a boat with one oar. You can keep yourself mighty busy just going around in circles.

"It's more important to do the right thing than to do things right."
—Peter F. Drucker

Don't overkill low priorities with excessive planning and energy. You don't need a sledgehammer to kill gnats. The amount of planning and energy you invest in an activity should be directly proportionate to the value of the outcome. Even though you want to pick up your laundry on the way home better than anyone else picks up their laundry, particularly because that's now the number-one priority on your list, it doesn't require quite as much pomp and circumstance as the presentation to the chairman of the board earlier that day.

Make sure that your first consideration is getting the right things done. After that, concentrate on how efficiently you're doing them. Row with both oars in the water. The difference between a failure and a success is two well-planned hours per day. Two well-planned hours out of 24 is not very much.

I've worked with many high achievers and wanna-be high achievers who dedicate themselves to time-planning only to sit down and plan a series of days that Superman, Captain Marvel, and Hopalong Cassidy couldn't pull off together. The eager over-achievers hit the bricks running and look terrific until, somewhere in the middle of the day, they burp.

The burp wasn't on their three-day plan and throws them so far behind schedule that they can't catch up. I advise people to start by planning two blockbuster hours a day. Over time you'll get more proficient and be able to plan half of the day with tightly scheduled activities. Work up to it and you won't be disillusioned that you can't become a miracle worker overnight.

I've never met a person who can effectively schedule more than 90 percent of his or her day. No matter how good you get to be at drafting and working priority lists, there will always be influences beyond your control. Stay flexible and you will spend less of your energy being frustrated and disappointed. High-performance people learn quickly that much of the day will be spent operating in the margins of their schedule.

"I always say to myself, 'What is the most important
thing we can think about at this extraordinary moment?"
—Buckminster Fuller

The T-R-A-F formula

In helping executives organize their activities for increased efficiency, Stephanie Winston also suggests that every item that comes over the transom be handled in one of four ways: *Trash, Refer, Action, or File.* High-performance people learn quickly that some items are simply not worth their time. These things have to be thrown out.

This doesn't mean throwing things away because you don't want to deal with them. To *trash* something because it helps you avoid responsibility is wrong. Something is eligible for the circular file only when the time and effort it requires don not move you closer to attaining any of your documented goals. In other words, when the item in question requires you to waste time, it's not worth pursuing. Develop the ability to discern quickly.

Referring or delegating an assignment to someone else is appropriate when the time and effort required are not worthy of your time according to the priority list you've established. What is down the list for you might be a noble cause for someone with less authority or less responsibility. Any efficient organization understands that items with varying priorities should be handled at different levels of the operation.

Action, in Winston's model, stands for things that *you* should do. Items could include calls *you* should return, letters *you* should write or visits *you* should make in person. When the items facing you represent top priorities for the accomplishment of your goals, there is nobody more appropriate than you to take care of them. *Action* means *you.*

Filing means storing information that you think might be helpful down the road. Filing something that will cause your plans to suffer if not attended to isn't wise. Only bits of information that don't require any immediate or even pending action on your part should be filed.

Be careful that filing doesn't become a method of delaying action on something that you merely want to avoid or postpone.

Stephanie Winston's *T-R-A-F* model is helpful because nothing you encounter requires anything other than one of the four treatments. Nothing should remain on your desk without receiving one of the four treatments. The high-performance person will do something with everything that comes his or her way without delay. That's how you can keep your decks cleared and ready for action at all times. The last thing you want to do is leave something critical undone because you're buried under unimportant matters.

Laying out a daily plan

1.The first thing to do in laying out a daily plan is to consider priorities. Distinguish between urgent and unimportant tasks.

Dwight Eisenhower said, "Urgent things are seldom important and important things are seldom urgent." Urgent tasks require immediate attention, but have little or no impact on the achievement of long-term goals. Important tasks are valuable in reaching the all-important long-term goals.

2.When laying out your daily plan, allow 10 percent more time for each task than you initially estimate it would take.

Allowing for the margins of your day gives you flexibility to adjust to the pace of the day. As I've mentioned, there will always be unexpected distractions and intrusions on your time. You want to avoid adding pressure to your day by scheduling your priority items too close together and forcing yourself to be constantly behind and playing catch up.

3.Strive to make the first hour of your day the most satisfying. Do the three things you want to do the least in your first hour.

It's better to get unpleasant tasks out of the way early so they don't hang over your head all day long. Having unpleasant things ahead of you tends to tarnish everything else you attempt. When the least pleasant tasks are dispatched early in the morning, the rest of the day will be a happier experience, no matter what you do.

Whether you're a morning or an afternoon person, you'll never have more natural energy throughout the day than you do in the morning. Many people feel as if they can't get going in the morning. Unfortunately, these folks are allowing the time when their minds and bodies are the most rested to be wasted. I suggest that you rise a half-hour early if you're a slow starter and go for a brisk walk before your morning shower. That way you'll be able to devote the most energized hours of your day to accomplishing difficult tasks that would be even more overwhelming later in the day.

4. Schedule your most important creative work during your personal best time of the day.

Despite the fact that your mind and body are most rested in the hours after you first wake up, every one has a different internal clock when it comes to the part of the day when s/he is most productive and creative. Call it your own personal *zone* if you wish. You ought to know by now what the most productive part of the day is for you. If not, pay attention to when you seem to get the most accomplished when you're not consciously thinking about it. When you're cranking out work a mile a minute and it doesn't even occur to you until you look back and say to yourself, "Wow, I don't remember doing all of that." For different folks that period of tremendous efficiency represents the best part of the day for creativity. It's a period when it just sort of all "happens" for you—a time when you're at your personal best. It occurs during the same part of the day, every day.

5. When a problem pops up, step back.

The natural inclination when an obstacle appears is to bull ahead with greater velocity. We all have a natural tendency to bear down harder on the square peg when it won't slip easily through the round hole. The truth is that a square peg shouldn't slip through a round hole unless somebody fiddled with the laws of physics while we weren't looking.

When a problem pops up and impedes our progress, there might be a good reason. Just pushing and pounding harder won't promote understanding and enlightenment. By stepping back from the problem, taking a longer view of it and grading its parts and priorities, you can move back in and start to solve the problem.

I learned about backing off from problems and letting naturally corrective forces take over when I was in the Air Force. The 22-ton fighter I was flying had a slight design flaw. If the aircraft reached a certain angle of climb, it was subject to a "pitch-up". A pitch-up meant losing control of the aircraft and possibly entering an uncontrollable tumble to the ground.

The Air Force had already told me not to worry about pitch-ups. There were systems designed into the aircraft to safeguard against the problem. I had learned early on that when the Air Force said not to worry about something, it was worth worrying about. Sure enough, I was doing practice target runs at a simulated high-flying intruder when my fighter went into a pitch-up. The systems, meant to safeguard against such things, failed.

I began to tumble out of the sky. The aircraft rolled so violently that the inside of the Plexiglas canopy was torn up by my crash helmet beating against it and had to be replaced. I tumbled out of control for over 30,000 feet (more than six miles). I was fighting like mad to pull the aircraft out of the tumble.

It felt like every drop of blood I had in my body was in my head. The negative "G's" inside the cockpit were so intense that all of the blood vessels in my eyes ruptured. This was more than the average problem that pops up around the office on a typical day. However, the principle that saved my life that day applies to the office as well as the physics of flight.

I finally figured out that bearing down harder on my problem and trying to force the controls of the aircraft wasn't going to work. Only three out of nine pilots who had experienced pitch-ups before me had survived. I didn't want to be doing whatever it was the six unlucky guys were doing when they hit the ground.

I neutralized the controls and released, popped the drag chute and lowered the landing gear. Suddenly the air began flowing over the wings again and the fighter stabilized all by itself. After all, those things are built to fly. I saved my life and several million in taxpayers' dollars

Task- Evaluation Sequence

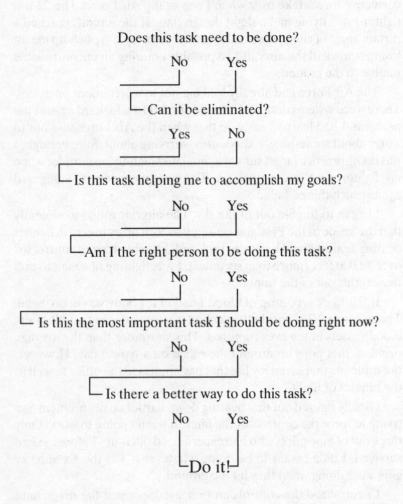

Figure 3.1

by backing off, just when my instincts drove me to press the situation harder.

So next time you feel like you're tumbling out of control, especially in a debate with someone else, back off the controls, pop your drag chute and let some natural stabilizing effects occur. If the best possible thing is to hammer harder, you can always do that later. For starters, make it your policy to step back and gain a broader and clearer perspective on the problem *first*.

6. Prior to each task, take a 30-second test.

The following questions only take a few moments to ask and answer. However, they will provide you with keen insight into how appropriate it is for you to be doing that particular task at that time. It might seem like I propose asking a great many questions and it's not hard to understand that concern. The value of putting things under the microscope as much as possible is not found in the questions, but rather in the answers.

The better-informed you are, the more likely your decisions are going to bring lasting benefits. That's why you want to take the time to evaluate your activities with the following inquisition:

1. Why is this task being done?
2. Can it be eliminated?
3. How is this task helping me achieve my goals?
4. Based upon what I've scheduled myself to earn (accomplish) this month, am I the one who should be doing this task?
5. Based on my established priorities, is this the most important task for me to be working on right now?
6. Is there a better way to do this task? How can I improve on the traditional method?

The time spent qualifying the things you do will result in freeing up more time for higher-priority tasks by shifting time away from tasks that are better done by others or not done at all. Figure 3.1

Project Sheet

Project	Date Assigned	Deadline	Date Completed

Figure 3.2

Meeting Planner

Name	Name	Name
Name	Name	Name
Name	Name	Name
		Name
Name	Name	Name
		Name

Figure 3.3

shows how this short question-answer process can liberate you to move to your next task at the first "yes" answer.

7. Never commit to a future assignment unless you have time for it now.

For some reason, the future always seems full of potential to do things that we just can't seem to accomplish now. In the correct context, that thought probably has some merit. Yet, the most common myth we buy into is that we will magically have some capability and/or capacity in the future that we don't presently possess. My friend Jim Newton comically referred to his future as "spotless." In truth our futures are spotless, but that's only because we haven't been there yet. Unless you are doing something specific now, over and above what you ordinarily do to make your methods more time-efficient, why would you think that you'll have more time in the future than you have right now?

Can you look back over the past few years and spot big holes where you had too little to do? Unless you have a history of encountering slow periods when you can take on extra projects and responsibilities, there's no reason to believe that you'll be able to in the next week, month, or year. The *high-performance process* will make you more efficient over time, but your future commitments should always be based on your present capabilities.

Learn to say no and mean it. It's more disrespectful to others to make promises you can't keep than it is to be honest up front. The desire to possess supernatural abilities is natural, but it's also a fantasy. No manager worth his or her salt expects you to work beyond your natural capacity. If you don't have time for a project now, you won't have time for it later. Trust me on that. Gauge future commitments on your present capacity to handle your workload.

8. Don't beat yourself up for not completing your priority list each day.

You can only do what your natural talents, knowledge, experience and circumstances allow. High-performance people know that working a priority list correctly means that their energies are always being spent on the number-one priority. Because of that, they're always filled with confidence knowing their efforts would not have been better allocated elsewhere.

If you're working your priority list correctly and have put each task to the 30-second test I described earlier, there are no items more important than the items you're working on. If anything needs to be left undone or pushed farther down the schedule, it should be the lower priority items.

You always want to finish every item on your list, but it's more important to focus on your priorities than the number of tasks you can scratch off. Many people procrastinate and avoid important, high-priority items by busying themselves with completing all sorts of less-important tasks. They appear to be constantly busy, and indeed they are. The high-performance person is constantly busy as well, but the value of his or her labors is far different.

If you're committed to the *high-performance process,* you're already aware that no other method of operation you might have subscribed to in the past would have made you any better able to complete every item on your priority list. When you're putting the high-performance methods and techniques I'm teaching you into practice, there's no need to fret over whether you're at your best. The *high-performance process* brings you to your highest performance level every day, and when you're not firing on all cylinders, you'll know why.

9. Carry pen and paper with you at all times.

Make it a part of your daily plan to be prepared for any opportunity to sketch out ideas. You never know when a good idea might hit and you'll want to pencil it out. It's also important to have a contingency plan for waiting time. If you're waiting for an appointment or for a meeting to start, there's no need to let your momentum slip. Have a secondary task staged and ready to go when some unexpected delay occurs.

10. Use your daily planner, to-do list, and project sheet.

Figures 3.2 and 3.3 are samples of planning tools that will help you focus your energies around the accomplishment of your documented goals. Some folks look at the use of planners as a waste of time. Any

Project Sheet
Interruption Log

Inter-ruption	Description	Time Begin/End	# of Minutes	Preventative Action to Be Taken
1				
2				
3				
4				
5				
6				
7				
8				
9				
10				
11				
12				
13				
14				

Figure 3.4

high-performance person will tell you that a few minutes spent planning will save hours in wasted effort in an unorganized day.

Combining your written planning as much as possible is always helpful, but planning your various types of activities will provide more specific help. For example, planning telephone conversations and planning conferences are similar activities. You should only use separate sheets and planners when the task calls for it.

Use the following code system to indicate what the priority ranking is for each item you list on your planning documents:

1. Do immediately.
2. Do by the end of the day.
3. Do today if possible.
4. Delegate.

How to handle interruptions

Interruptions are inevitable but not unmanageable. One of the primary reasons for scheduling margins in your day of 10 percent or more is to accommodate unscheduled activities. One of the most common mistakes among people who have a busy agenda is to focus too much attention on what happens to fall in front of them or whoever might drop in or call.

These types of interruptions that contaminate your time are instigated by others. When other people determine how your time is spent, you lose control. More than that, when other people are allowed to dictate how you spend your time, they, not you, are establishing your priorities. High-performance people accept that interruptions are bound to occur and they anticipate them. However, high-performance people have a plan to keep interruptions from stealing or undermining their control.

Step one in handling interruptions is to *rearrange your office* by relocating your desk where you will no longer be in the line of sight of those passing by. It's too easy for people to make eye contact with you as they pass by in the hall and simply walk in to socialize. As soon as that happens, you're confronted with the distracting and time-consuming task of politely excusing yourself so that you can return to work.

There's nothing wrong with social interaction during the day—in fact a healthy rapport with your associates is valuable. However, socializing must be kept in perspective and always on your terms according to the priorities and schedule you've established. There are times when higher-ups will make social demands on your time and you'll be hard-pressed to maneuver your way around them. But that's where your personal talent, knowledge, and experience come in handy. People use the discussion of all sorts of ostensive business problems as excuses to kill time, theirs and yours. Procrastination loves company. You don't want to be that company.

Reduce the number of chairs in your office and keep the remaining ones as far from your desk as possible. Don't create an appealing nuisance by fashioning a conversation pit right in front of you. A cozy conversation area is another incentive to socialize. When you do elect to take time to carry on a discussion with a visitor, get up from behind your desk and move around to one of the chairs yourself.

If the discussion is important enough for you to leave your desk and focus all of your attention on your guest, it must be a high-priority task. If it's not important enough for you to move, it's probably a discussion that's robbing a high-priority task of your attention. It's easy to talk and talk, hoping to cover some important ground somewhere in the conversation. The high-performance person knows where the important ground is and goes there immediately or, realizing the lack of value in a conversation, excuses himself or herself quickly.

When you are in conversation with someone in your office, relocate the clock relative to the chairs so that both you and the other party can see it. A casual glance at the clock is a subtle reminder that valuable time is passing. More than one glance at the clock is a pretty unmistakable cue that it's time to move on.

If the other person doesn't take the hint, no matter how obvious, look at the clock and say, "I see it's time that I get back to work on my priority job for the day," or something to that effect. Then stand up and move back to your desk. Your movement is a physical gesture to support your verbal comment about getting back to work.

If necessary, complete the conversation while walking the visitor back to the reception area or back to his or her desk. In this way, *you* become the person with the prerogative to leave when you so choose, which will be promptly. Never sit and wonder to yourself, "When is this person ever going to let me get back to work?" You determine when you go back to work.

Step two in handling interruptions is to *keep an interruption log* for one week. (Fig. 3.4) I know that it's another time-consuming bother, but the educational value can be tremendous. This isn't something to do constantly. The point is to illustrate the impact interruptions are having on your time. Once you've seen on paper the scope of your interruptions, it's easier to get fired up about eliminating or minimizing their debilitating effect on your performance.

Step three in handling interruptions is to *establish a quiet hour* when you will not be interrupted, no matter what. I've found that during a quiet hour, I can get the equivalent of two or three hours of work done. Having a quiet hour set-aside during the day will provide you with a boost if you feel your productivity lagging behind.

Step four in handling interruptions is to *say no when someone asks if you have a minute.* This doesn't mean cut yourself off from other people or be rude. However, it's important to establish with your fellow workers the necessity to plan ahead. If someone needs some help or information, they will be willing to come back at the top of the hour or whenever you're at a logical stopping place. When s/he returns at the designated time, deal with the issue s/he originally came to you about and deal with nothing else.

Step five in handling interruptions is to *reverse the tide.* When someone has a habit of coming into your office, seeking advice or help, look up and ask him or her what s/he thinks is best. If it sounds feasible, offer affirmation and encouragement and then drop your head and get back to work. Again, this is not permission to be rude, but a way to quickly dismiss an invitation to waste valuable time.

Step six in handling interruptions is to avoid being a part of the problem. Some "problems" are not only unimportant, they're much less of a problem than you might think, given the number of people dropping everything to work on it. High-performance people know how to apply the 30-second test to a problem and quickly determine whether it's worth their time and attention. When a problem is not worth getting entangled in, or it's really not a problem at all, you must have the ability to concentrate and not be distracted by all the clamor going on around you.

Getting off the telephone...fast

You already know that one of the biggest time-wasters in your life is the telephone. Here are some ways to consciously control the time you spend on the telephone, based on these techniques originally developed by Stephanie Winston:

1. Preset the time limit. When someone calls to talk about an issue, immediately tell that person how much time you can spend in telephone conversation. This means that you need to determine quickly how much time you feel is appropriate for that subject in light of your priorities. Once you've determined the appropriate amount of time, say something like, "Yes, I can spend three minutes with you on that." As soon as you've designated a specific time frame for the conversation, the caller must focus on the issue and not babble aimlessly.

2. Foreshadow endings. When someone calls you on the telephone and takes a long time getting to the point, a little reminder that your time is limited might help him or her focus. For example, as you notice that the caller is not focusing, you might say, "Before we hang up I want to be sure I've answered the question you called about."

    Your comment communicates your sincere attempt to be helpful while, at the same time, making it clear that the conversation is not open-ended and will soon be over. It's a courteous method of drawing the telephone conversation to an end.

3. Use *their* time. Whenever someone is being especially talkative on the telephone and doesn't seem to be getting the message that your time is valuable, tell the person that you're in the middle of an urgent project and ask if you can call back.

   When you call back, make sure it's just before that person's quitting time. That way s/he will place a value on the matter relative to his or her desire to get out of the office. In the vast majority of cases, I believe you'll find the matter wasn't all that important to begin with.

4. Use the other person's estimate. When someone calls and asks if you have time to discuss something, immediately ask how long you think the discussion will require and then suggest less time. If someone says they think it will take 10 minutes to discuss something, say, "Let's try to do it in five."

   Once again, you're not refusing to spend time helping the caller. You're just establishing parameters on how much time you're willing to invest. In the long run you're not only protecting your own valuable time, but also helping the other party focus his or her energies.

5. Change focus. If it appears that your time is being wasted on unimportant matters and the other caller is difficult to reason with, steer the conversation toward your own problems. Ask questions that the caller can't answer.

   The purpose of shifting focus from the caller's problems to your own is to take the fun out of it for the caller. When a person is going on and on about his or her own issues, it can be an extremely narcissistic episode. One thing a narcissist never wants to do is share the spotlight.

6. Get help. If you can't get someone off of the phone easily or if the person is too important to risk offending in any way, have your secretary or someone working close to you call you on another extension, giving you an excuse to terminate the first call.

7. Use your conference planner. When you're the one initiating the call, don't fall into the same time-wasting traps
   that others subject you to. Plan your calls before you
   make them. Note what you want to discuss and how long
   you realistically feel it should take. Out of respect for
   your own time and others' time, stick to your plan as
   closely as possible.

Learning from emergencies

There once was a man who drank liquor to excess and was booted
out of the local tavern every night at closing time. As a shortcut home,
he staggered through the village graveyard in the dark.

Although he knew his way among the gravestones fairly well, he
wasn't aware one night that a fresh open grave had been dug earlier
that afternoon in preparation for a funeral the following day. He fell
into the hole.

The inebriated man tried and tried again to scale the vertical walls
of the grave with no success. Finally accepting the futility of his situation, he sat down in a corner of the pit and decided to sleep until
morning when someone would surely discover him.

Later that night a traveler who had lost his bearings wandered
into the same cemetery and promptly fell into the same open grave. In
the pitch-blackness, the traveler wasn't aware of his drunken com-
panion sleeping it off in the corner.

As the traveler tried again and again to scale the sheer walls of the
neatly dug grave without success, the drinker woke up and noticed
that someone else was in a similar predicament to his.

Unfamiliar with his surroundings, the traveler called out for help
several times. There was no response. Slumping into an opposite corner of the grave, he felt alone, helpless and scared.

Wanting to comfort the new arrival, the drinker spoke up. "It's
no use, you can't get out." An instant later the inebriated man was
alone again in the grave.

Just when you think there is no faster way to get a job done, an emergency will arise and somehow, some way, you'll get it done much faster. How could that be? It's the same task and you're the same person. Although every situation is different, the lesson to be learned is that virtually anything can be done by virtually anyone in a state of emergency faster than it would be done under normal circumstances.

I'm not suggesting that you pull a fire alarm every time production slows down. A high-performance person is aware of how much his or her capabilities seem to increase under pressure and has that increased capacity in the back of his or her mind at all times. It can be a confidence-building technique, knowing that you can do a great deal more if need be. It also keeps you aware that you might be doing less than you could be in a normal operating environment.

How would you be doing your job if a medical problem arose and forced you to cut your workday by half? If you had no other choice but to try and salvage as much of your productivity as possible under altered conditions, how would you go about it? The answers to these questions will tell you a great deal about your present working habits.

Would there be parts of your job that you would drop completely without diminishing the end result? Which tasks would you delegate to others so that the end result is not diminished? Which people would you avoid because the drain they place on your time would detract from the precious little time you have left? I've never met anyone who couldn't shed some dead weight off of his or her routine and maintain—if not improve—productivity.

Reading faster

Reading, as important as it is, can slow you down if you don't do it with the same intensity and purpose that you use to execute your other responsibilities. The way you approach work-related reading is quite different from the way you read for pleasure. Work-related reading is a search for relevant and useful information as quickly as possible.

Speed-reading experts say to move your finger or a pencil under the words as fast as you can and force your eye to keep up with it. Your brain can input visual data much faster than you would customarily ask it to. Bear in mind that you're searching for ideas, not individual words. Moving your finger or a pencil under the words will have the immediate effect of doubling your reading rate. If you practice this method with your daily reading, you will soon be able to jump your finger or pencil down the page.

You can begin picking up entire ideas that the writer has formed using words and sentences without poring over the words and sentences themselves. The more you use speed-reading techniques, the more proficient you will become and the more information you will retain.

Handling paperwork

Keeping your desk and mind clear for the high-priority tasks is an integral part of your planning process. You won't keep your decks cleared by accident. If you find yourself bogged down by telephone calls, handling the mail or paperwork in general, it's because methods and techniques for steering clear of these distractions were not given their rightful place in your high-performance strategy.

There are new beliefs you need to adopt as well as new habits and behaviors. The following list applies to handling paperwork:

1. You don't have to read everything that comes across your desk or arrives in the mail.

This piece of news sounds astonishing to many people who feel as if they're somehow obligated to examine everything that someone mailed to them or routed in their direction. You can live very well without the vast majority of correspondence that flows through your life.

Develop the habit of scanning things very quickly to determine if the correspondence is something related to a current project, generated by someone important to your objectives, or of some potential future value to your documented goals. In the latter case, you'll probably visit your files of delayed correspondence from time to time and pitch most of them when you realize they didn't have much value after all.

By quickly filing the correspondence for later review in the first place, you saved yourself the wasted time of contemplating the possible relevance of the information when you had higher-priority fish to fry. Like the telephone, meticulously scrutinizing the mail and every item in your inbox can be a time-wasting tool for procrastinators.

2. Preview materials for key words and phrases.

Even faster than speed reading, this technique helps you make a virtually instantaneous appraisal of the document and its value to you and your objectives. If you spot something that's relevant, go back and give it a closer skimming using the speed-reading techniques I described earlier. As always, your goal is to make a rapid determination of how the document fits into your current high-performance strategy.

3. Organize your paper work according to priority.

As you determine what items you're going to deal with yourself, delegate to others, spread them out according to the priority ranking you've assigned them. Processing the material that comes across your desk without organizing it in an accessible fashion means that you'll duplicate part of your effort later when you go digging to see what needs to be attended to.

4. Never pick up a piece of paper unless you intend to do something with it.

If you don't resolve that you're going to take action on something before you pick it up, you're wasting your time looking at it. If you catch yourself reaching for something on your desk, quickly ask yourself if you have the time and inclination to do whatever will be required to dispatch that item and move on to something else. If you don't, then don't pick it up. It's just that simple.

If the doubting voice in your head is saying, "How am I going to know if it's important?" you haven't prioritized your paper flow the way I suggested in the previous items. If it's on your desk at all, you've already determined that it's a priority and you have a sense of what level of effort will be required to handle it.

Therefore, if you reach for it, you must be prepared to deal with it. Otherwise you're just piddling around. When you reach for an item, you're triggering your focus mechanism. By virtue of the fact you've selected that item to deal with, you've ranked it as your number-one priority at that moment and it deserves your complete attention and energy.

Realistically, not every task can be completed in one effort before going on to the next. If that's the case, put a red dot in the upper right-hand corner of the paper each time you set it down. The red dots will give you an instant assessment of how often you're returning to that task to make progress. It's good information to know in case you're spending more time and effort on the issue than it deserves.

5. Plan your response method.

My favorite method of responding to someone's communication is to write my comments right on the original document and send it back. I also make a copy and file it in order to keep a record of the written exchange. In other cases, I'll have a form response prepared for items that appear frequently and require a stock reply.

I prefer the former method because writing on someone's original document gives the impression that you've seen it, handled it and that it got your attention. If you're concerned that folks might feel you didn't care enough to draft a letter or memo to respond to their letter or memo, have a rubber stamp made that says, "Hand-written reply for immediate response. Copy on file." If the originator of the document wants to call and discuss the matter further, s/he knows that you have both copies of the original and your response on file.

Using the form letter or paragraph to respond is definitely less personal and, as such, can be appropriate when the correspondence you're responding to is annoying or trivial. Much of your mail is unnecessary and tedious. In such cases, when the tedious material arrives regularly, a form response will save you time and convey your opinion of the matter's urgency or value.

Be considerate of others' time

To some folks, the methods and techniques I recommend that you include in your planning process for minimizing distractions, interruptions and saving time seem impersonal. On the contrary, I've found in my career that people appreciate brevity and straightforward behavior. I certainly carry out my tasks in a respectful and friendly manner.

Just because you plan timesaving efficiency techniques into the execution of your responsibilities doesn't mean that you have to be abrasive. In my experience, most of the abrasive and rude people I encounter are precisely those who need to adopt some time-saving techniques. It's usually those who are overwhelmed by the unnecessary pressures brought on by chaos and disorganization who tend to bite your head off.

Brevity is the essence of good communications. If someone is a busy, hard-working person, s/he will appreciate your brevity. Try to boil your ideas and comments down to less than a minute if possible. Someone once told me to, "Speak in headlines. If the listener wants to hear more, give 'em the text." If an idea that you want to communicate is well thought-out, you will have already formed headlines.

In the same way that you scan printed information for the larger ideas and concepts, you should communicate with others by beginning with the overview and stating the central message clearly and succinctly. Even if your time is not limited, making your basic point quick, and easy to grasp, makes your message easier to follow. Nobody enjoys being confused.

An "interruptee" can also become an "interrupter." Are you part of the problem? When someone interrupts you, it's possible to ignore the time-efficiency techniques you've learned and drag the conversation down all kinds of meaningless avenues. If someone agrees to abide by the time restrictions you request when you're interrupted, do you turn around and violate their time by not listening effectively and hogging the conversation?

Be prompt. Don't keep people waiting. Being respectful of other people's time will always be appreciated. If you've agreed to see someone and deal with issues s/he brings to your attention, don't delay. Show the other person respect by honoring his or her commitment to see you and respect your own time by handling the issue as expeditiously as possible. Because promptness is as much a benefit to you as it is to the other party, it makes sense to be prompt with anyone, not just those people you feel are important. Any behavior that's worth making an extra effort for should be part of your regular routine. Wouldn't you want to be known as a person who is prompt, courteous and respectful of others?

Your personal time effectiveness affects the productivity of others. That's true even if no one else reports to you. How efficient you are with your time has a profound impact on everyone around you. It's a good idea to periodically ask people under your supervision how you can help their time efficiency. Ask them, "What do I do that consumes your time without contributing to your effectiveness?" Then change accordingly.

How to recharge your enthusiasm

It's important that your planning process include provisions for the inevitable drain on your enthusiasm. You know that any major effort will require energy, and periods of intense focus on an issue will take something out of you. Don't think that you can simply bull your way through one task and move directly to another without any loss in enthusiasm or energy.

Plan some quiet time alone. Make it part of your overall strategy. Know going in that, after you've given your best effort to a task, you will have a period of peace and quiet to reflect on what you just did, to ponder what lies ahead, or to not think of anything at all. Having your rejuvenation included in your plan makes the effort seem less overwhelming.

Break a job down. By taking a big task and breaking it down into smaller tasks you automatically engage a sense of accomplishment at the completion of each smaller task instead of staying frustrated at the enormity of the overall challenge. Being happier along the way keeps your enthusiasm and energies up. Keeping your enthusiasm and energies up will speed the accomplishment of the bigger chore.

Reward yourself for completing tough jobs. By building the reward into your original plan, you will have a constant sense of what the job is worth to you on a personal level. Too often you can appreciate the professional accomplishment without personalizing any unique benefit. Knowing there is a carrot out there that's been budgeted as part of the process helps the medicine of hard work go down easier.

Take a break. Plan to pause at midday or other appropriate time to let your body and brain load up on oxygen again. If your refreshment breaks are not included in your original plan, it will feel like even going to the restroom means falling behind. Breaks are inevitable. You'll take some whether you plan them or not. You might as well plan on them to have better control and to properly exploit the benefits of periodic rests.

Plan where you will go and when. Going to lunch or walking in the park have different effects on different people. Which is better for you in light of the task you face? Knowing in advance that you're going to pause in your effort helps you come back to the job with renewed vigor. Your thoughts during a planned time off tend to be creative, free-flowing concepts that might contribute much to the task at hand.

Make somebody else happy. In the play *Cheaper By The Dozen,* the father calculated that most people are awake for 16 hours per day. Out of that 960 minutes, 1 percent should be spent making someone else happy. There's nothing like getting outside of yourself to recharge your batteries. When all of your focus remains inward, it's easy to lose perspective and think that the problems of the world are greater than they really are. Planning to spend some time, even a small amount of time, brightening someone else's day will help you keep your task in perspective and improve your personal performance.

Know when to stop for the day

If stopping places are part of your strategy, you will not debate in your own mind whether to press on a little further. On a job that requires an extended amount of time to complete, you know that you'll have to stop each day anyway. So plan your stopping places in advance and avoid the problems of deciding how far to go.

Just as breaking a large job down into smaller parts gives you more chances to experience a feeling of accomplishment, granting yourself advanced permission to end each day at a reasonable hour tends to alleviate guilt. The close of a workday will begin to feel like an accomplishment because you've structured your progress in appropriate segments.

When you've stopped at a preplanned spot, you'll return the next day with increased energy, eager to take on the job once again, knowing that you'll feel good at the end of another productive day. When it's not possible to predict where you'll be at the end of each day, make sure that you choose to end on a high note. A good feeling as you leave the job sets the stage for good feelings as you return. Note the specific phrase or calculation that you'll begin with upon your return.

If you are forced to stop when you're stalled on an unresolved problem, take a moment to write the problem out in simple, clear-cut terms. By focusing both your creative right brain and your linear (writing) left brain on the problem before you break, you will unleash creative powers in your unconscious that will work on the problem even when you're not consciously thinking about it.

I suggested earlier in the section to have pen and paper with you at all times. Be prepared to write down creative solutions that might come to you at any time. When your unconscious mind is searching for solutions, you never know when they'll come or what they'll be.

The worst thing you can do is stimulate your creativity to find an answer, only to forget it shortly after it pops into your head.

Finally, clear your desk every night, leaving only one high-priority item waiting for you when you return. While you might have a number of high-priority tasks ahead of you, having them all greet you first thing in the morning can be a disincentive. You can only effectively work on one at a time anyway. So pick your most pressing chore and get after it with all the energy and vitality you bring with you at the start of the new day.

The same technique holds true for lunch breaks. Before you go to lunch, clear away everything except that one big job that you want to jump into with both feet as soon as you return. The point is to get those high-priority jobs out of the way as soon as possible. Identifying them before you break means the most energized moments upon your return will be spent solving the problem, not deciding which problem to solve.

Launching the Plan

"All things come to those who wait provided they hustle while they wait."

—Thomas A. Edison

My wife and I were passengers in a hot air balloon early one African morning. As the balloon rose gracefully, we saw a herd of wildebeest running frantically across the vast expanse below us. The herd stopped suddenly and began looking around as if they were confused. We asked our pilot/guide why the herd had stopped so suddenly and what they were looking for.

He told us that the wildebeest, which migrate by the millions across grassy African plains, are not good learners. An entire herd will take flight at the slightest indication of danger. They will run wildly for a short time and then stop, forgetting why they began running in the first place.

According to our local expert, the lions, who are good learners, simply follow the stampeding wildebeest herd at a leisurely pace and wait for them to stop. When the wildebeest forget why the herd was running, it's dinnertime for the lions. Our guide said that wildebeest are so memory-challenged that they will even walk up to a sleeping lion and sniff at it. The lion wakes up and has breakfast in bed.

The wildebeest remind me of people who lose focus and/or lose direction by not following their plan. These folks remember that they had a plan once, but can't remember what it was or why it was important. As you launch your plan into action, the plan must remain your central focus and purpose. Only then will all of your hustle and energy be concentrated on achieving your documented goals. The subject is action.

Anticipation without action breeds frustration.
Frustration breeds disillusionment.

The reason I set this statement apart is to demonstrate that launching a plan is a critical link in the *high-performance process*. Many people give up on planning, not because they have any problems completing that phase of the process, but because they can't seem to get started on the *action* phase. As a result, their plans, which produce great anticipation, never see the light of day and the net result is frustration.

The more frustrated you get, the more disillusioned you become. The more disillusioned you become, the more powerless and less motivated you feel. In the end, it doesn't make sense to plan any more if you can't expect to see any results. All of this is under your control, of course. That's why it's important to devote a section to *launching your plan*.

Sweaty palms

Someone once advised me to live every day as if it were my last day on Earth because one day I would be right. Wouldn't it be a shame to get to the last day you have on Earth and say, "Wait· a minute, I never did any of those things I planned to do"? By then, it's too late. Launching the plan means transforming *thinking* into *action*.

Thinking and planning are one thing, but actually getting up and *doing* is something else. There is little threat of anything changing in your life if all you do is sit around and think about things. The thought of actually taking initiative to make things happen is enough to give you sweaty palms. As I've mentioned before, your actions speak with a louder and more credible voice than do your thoughts and words.

When you take the initiative to make something happen by putting your plans into action, things will change. It's impossible for your life to stay the same while you exert effort toward the attainment of a goal. If you *think* you're working toward a goal and nothing is changing, you're probably doing a lot more *thinking* than *acting*.

Loren Janes is the stunt person who doubled for the actress playing the role of Jill Kinmont in the film *The Other Side of the Mountain.* In shorthand that means he took a 50-foot fall on skis, off the side of a mountain, on purpose, to simulate the accident that left Jill partially paralyzed. He fell and the cameras rolled.

I asked Loren if he still gets sweaty palms before he does a major "gag" (movie-biz lingo for a stunt). "Danny," he replied, "if I don't get sweaty palms, I don't do the gag." At first blush, that sounds like you should only do things that make you nervous. That's partially what Loren meant. If you're not doing something that makes your palms sweat, you're not stretching yourself very far.

On the other hand, you can attempt something outrageous and even dangerous and convince yourself that it's really not a big deal. If Loren steps up to do a challenging stunt with dry palms, he knows right away that he's not mentally prepared and he backs off lest he blow the attempt and/or injure himself. The same goes for you and me. When *thinking* becomes *doing,* sweaty palms indicate that we're embarking on a true adventure—and in touch with reality.

> *"Life is either a daring adventure or nothing."*
>
> —Helen Keller

Those are profound words from a woman who was rendered deaf, mute, and blind by a serious illness in her infancy. Helen Keller was never expected to develop the ability to communicate with others, much less become an inspiration to the world. Nevertheless she did. Thank goodness someone who was never expected to understand life as a normal human being was able to get the message to us that, as a rule, we take life's opportunities too lightly.

Helen Keller's message is that life can either be an adventure or it can be a holding pattern until death. The choice belongs to each one of us. Creativity expert and author, Roger von Oech, uses a tombstone as an illustration in his book, *A Whack On The Side Of The Head*. The tombstone bears the inscription:

> *Here lies So-and-So.*
> *Died at the age of 30.*
> *Buried at the age of 70.*

Helen Keller was so grateful for the opportunity to live fully that she savored every moment and didn't let precious time slide by uneventfully. That meant she had to be an active person. Von Oech is telling us the same thing. Once you stop being active, you're as good as dead, even if you don't physically expire for another 40 years.

How many people do you know who are walking zombies? Are you a walking zombie? I'm convinced that zombies can actually be great planners. They simply stop at the planning stage and never do anything that would initiate change in their lives. Without change there can be no adventure outside of the terror you feel while being swept away by circumstance beyond your control.

The emotional death that von Oech refers to is insidious. It creeps up on you so slowly that you don't even realize you're dead. It's complacency that kills you. A nonadventurous, passive existence will suffocate whatever spark you once had inside. For most adults, all you have to do is ask what's the difference between how they feel about life now and how they remember feeling about life in their early 20s.

During early adulthood, life was constantly changing. Everything you did was a challenge. Change and activity stimulated your creativity and zest for life. People who stay excited about life and passionate about what they do right into their senior years are active people. They're doers. Those are not the folks watching the parade go by, they *are* the parade.

Before you write this off to hype and motivation, think of the practical application of this knowledge. I have already established that it's your uniqueness that brings meaning to your personal and professional lives. More than meaning, your unique talents, knowledge and experiences are what fuel excellence in everything you do.

As you stand at your personal crossroads in your personal moment of truth, can you honestly say that you don't want to be a mover and a shaker? If you told the truth, the whole truth, and nothing but the truth, so help you God, would you say, "I really don't want to be in the parade. I'd rather just watch, thank you."

Do you really expect to be given a more powerful and influential position based upon your lack of initiative? Should your employer or customers realistically give you more money for doing less? Just because the federal government can get away with that doesn't mean you should aspire to such contradictory standards. If you're not in a government job, you'd better become an adventure-seeker if you want to thrive and prosper.

Self-talk

Both low achievers and high achievers talk to themselves. The difference is what they say. Low achievers and high achievers have both discussed at length with themselves how quickly they each adapt to a new idea and how well they perform their daily tasks. Therein lies the problem or the progress. What does your self-talk do for you?

For starters, your internal dialogue has shaped your self-image. Your self-image controls your performance level—that is, how well you do your job. It's a cycle (See Fig. 4.1). Self-talk informs self-image and self-image dictates performance. As a child, did you ever spin the little merry-go-round at the park as fast as you could and then try to jump on?

That's much the same challenge as breaking into the self-talk cycle. It's hard to break into. But break in you must if you're to exert any control over your productivity; much less change it. A high-performance person knows that it's not *how* you break into the cycle, but *where* you break in that matters. Many people expend a great deal of energy trying to hop on the merry-go-round at the self-image or productivity stages.

If you've tried to improve your self-image or increase your productivity without lasting success, it's probably because you didn't break into your cycle at the self-talk stage. The self-talk stage is where it all begins and that's the only place that you can influence self-image or personal performance. You know what you're saying to yourself day-in and day-out. In fact you're the only one who can hear it.

Self-Talk Cycle

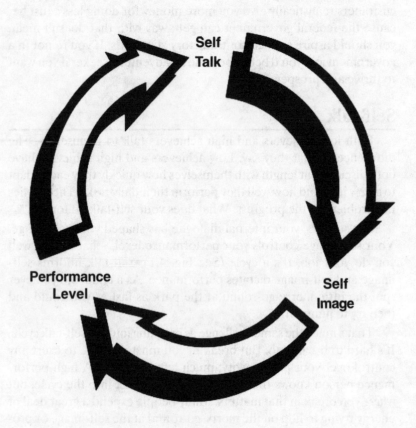

Figure 4.1

Others can observe your productivity and sense your self-image, but you're the only one who can hear the internal dialogue. You're also the only person who can change the dialogue. Encouraging yourself rather than beating yourself up will produce remarkable results as far as self-image and personal productivity are concerned. Sincere encouragement peps anybody up. Why would you be any different?

If you're not familiar with your internal dialogue, listen. You speak out loud in a clear, articulate voice in your head. You don't speak a foreign language (unless you're trying to be cute) and you don't speak in code. There's no excuse for not hearing what you say to yourself unless you're avoiding the subject. Make a note on your daily planner to listen to yourself.

Make a note at various times throughout the day to pause for a moment, just a moment, and hear the words. You might be amazed. At times when you're under tremendous pressure, listen to yourself. At times when you score a victory, listen to yourself. Just after someone really ticks you off or when you really do something stupid, listen to yourself.

If what you hear is negative, tell your internal voice that negativity isn't going to make anything better. Put in an encouraging word and get back to work. Have you ever seen a professional athlete, Olympic figure skater, or gymnast put in a good performance while screaming at him or herself?

The first thing trainers encourage their performers to do when negative thoughts emerge is to "shake them off" and once again visualize the positive images of attaining the desired rewards. Nobody knows better than superstar performers that self-talk is the control point for performance.

Understanding motivation

Motivation is probably the most corrupted word in the English language. It is so overused and improperly used that it's become synonymous with hype. I agree that much of what's passed off as motivation these days is little more than *hype*. When I talk about motivation, I'm talking about the no-monkey-business, honest-to-goodness, dictionary definition.

To motivate is to provide with a motive a reason to do something. Motivation is the by-product of desire. Desire and motivation are joined at the hip. Neither can exist in the absence of the other. They exist at the same level. No matter what your job responsibilities are, your desire for the rewards for a job well-done will be an exact match for your motivation level to do the job well.

The next time someone tells you that they want this or that so badly they can taste it, ask that person what it will take to get the object of his or her desire. If s/he knows what's required, ask if s/he is willing to do what it takes. It doesn't take much to figure out that we all do what's necessary to get whatever we want, provided we truly want it badly enough. If we don't have what we want, it's probably because, in reality, we don't want it as badly as we say we do.

Actions speak louder than words. If you want to know what's most important to someone, watch what s/he does. If it's important to know someone's real motivation, watch his or her behavior. Where his or her motivation is, so too will his or her desire be found. Have you fallen into the trap of saying, "I've been planning to do this or that for the longest time?"

The stepping-off place between planning and launching your plan into action is at your motivation level. A plan that remains indefinitely on the launching pad isn't within the planner's sincere desire. Any attempt to verbally convince you otherwise is just talk. The planner's energy would be better spent in constructive self-talk than in trying to convince someone else that s/he really wants that thing for which s/he hasn't seen fit to invest the necessary effort.

Levels of motivation

There are four levels to motivation (See Fig. 4.2). You're at one of the levels. If you have people working for you, every one of them is at one of the levels. Every human being in control of his or her faculties is at one of the levels. Each level represents a motive for action, ranging from the least encouraging motivation (level one) to the highest level of encouragement.

Motivation Levels
and Mental Mood Chart

Levels of Motivation		Mental Mood of
4.	Self-Motivation	Self-Confidence
3.	Commitment	Intuition
2.	Goal Identification	Reason
1.	Compliance	Desperation

Figure 4.2

Level 1 (lowest): Compliance

Do it or else. Few people enjoy working under these conditions. Nevertheless, the most frequently invoked management imperative is to do what you're told. Maybe that's because one of the most frequently invoked parental imperative is, "Do it because I told you to." The timeless logic to back that one up is the equally infamous, "Because I said so, that's why."

When you join the military, you're temporarily placing your other levels of motivation on the shelf, at least initially. In an organization that demands ultimate compliance, regimen, and cloning in the name of efficiency, that's where you always begin. When the mongrel hordes are descending upon you with death in their eyes, it's not a good time for management to form a task force to study the problem.

In civilian, that is to say *civilized*, society, compliance is the least productive form of motivation and the most resented. Why? Because it forbids the injection of your unique self into the equation. If bringing your unique talents, knowledge and experience to the job leads to the highest possible productivity, keeping your unique qualities under lock and key is destined to result in the worst productivity.

In a word, compliance, as a means of providing motive, is counterproductive. The first major office I managed as a civilian after leaving the Air Force was nearly destroyed by you-know-who. I managed to take my company's leading sales office, full of leading salespeople, and bring it down to number 36 out of 36 offices in three months. I had a knack for de-motivating people and I worked it to perfection.

What was my secret? Compliance. "Say it the way I say it, do it the way I do it and we'll all get along just fine." Believe it or not, little napoleonic autocrats, like I was in those days, don't demand conformity solely out of a need for power. There is seemingly sound logic behind cloning everyone in the organization after your own image.

I figured that if I could get everyone to think and behave just like me, they wouldn't bring me any problems that I hadn't already learned how to solve. Moreover, if I was so terrific that the company wanted me to manage the top office, then I must be doing things right. Right? If my behavior pleases the company brass, then what could be better than cloning everybody in the office to think and act exactly like me?

Character is not built at the compliance level. However, resentment flourishes. As parents we know that the sooner a child is brought into the decision-making process, the greater his or her compliance will become. The longer a child is told to blindly comply with orders, the greater his or her resistance becomes. Adults are like that, too. Except that adults are less forgiving than children are.

If an adolescent is told to move a box in the garage three feet, s/he will ask why. If the answer is, "Because I told you so," you'll be amazed at how much damage a box can sustain being moved only three feet. Actually the box is only getting the treatment you would get if the kid could get away with it. And you wonder why people at work are not more careful and conscientious with company property.

Level 2: Goal identification

If you want to generate animosity and resentment, operate on level one and demand compliance. If you want to begin building character, move up to level two where the objective is identification with the goal. That's all the adolescent is asking for when s/he asks why the box needs to be moved.

You're the one assigning the task. Therefore, you're the one who must provide the motive. You should know that people have a natural desire to identify with the goal and a natural resistance to being told to "do it or else." All you have to do is monitor your own feelings. You can feel the difference between being ordered to comply and being included in the reasoning behind an instruction—why should anyone else be different?

This is easy stuff. If you hate operating under compliance, you'd better believe everyone else does too. If you feel better about following instructions if you're informed about the objective, everyone else does too. You will put a plan into action with much more energy and enthusiasm if you identify with the goal. Even if you don't agree with the goal, knowing the desired outcome makes any task easier to deal with.

If you don't want to know the reasoning behind an assignment because you strongly disagree with the outcome, then you have an ethical dilemma that needs to be addressed. Why are you engaged in something that contradicts your beliefs in the first place? If you face such a challenge, it's time to return to your moment of truth and ask the hard questions.

Even if there's no direct benefit to you, it's still important to identify with the goal. At a core level, simply *agreeing* with the wisdom behind what's to be accomplished will heighten your motivation. It's hard to find a worthwhile task that doesn't, in some way, benefit everyone involved. When the adolescent understands that a clean garage contributes to the efficiency of the household and an efficient household has more time for fun things, goal identification becomes personal.

If you're the one providing motive to others, make sure that if you predict benefits from completed tasks, those benefits are realized. If you sell a lot of blue sky and don't deliver, you're doing nothing more than manipulating others and soon you won't have any alternative but to try and enforce compliance. When people feel exploited, their performance is bound to be worse than unmotivated.

In the same way that the box was damaged by a resentful helper, a person motivated by goal identification will not only move it, but dust it off to boot. Despite bearing the brunt of countless jokes in our day, Napoleon was a great leader in his day. He embraced and employed the concept of goal identification as he led thousands of troops on his military campaigns.

Napoleon said, "A great leader is a merchant of hope." Isn't the same thing true of parents? How about teachers? Anyone who successfully provides motive to others is a merchant of hope who communicates to others that their labors really do pay off after all. People naturally hope that they will have some personal investment in anything they're involved in. The desire to have your natural talents, knowledge, and experience recognized as part of the big picture is a tremendous motivator.

Level 3: Commitment

The only way personal motive can become stronger than identifying with a goal is to *internalize* the goal. In the same way that your personal talents, knowledge, and experience make anything you do more exciting, a goal is never more enthusiastically pursued than when it becomes part of you. Your level of personal investment is at its peak when you're genuinely committed to achieving your desired rewards.

High-performance people operate at level three and four. When folks are motivated by personal commitment, you'd best step out of their way unless you want footprints running up your back and down your front. The *high-performance process* of bringing as much of your talents, knowledge, and personal experience to the job as possible plops you right in the highest levels of motivation.

When you commit to a goal by internalizing it, you commit your strengths to the task. You bring all that's the best of you to the table. The adolescent who is motivated by identification with the goal of having more time for the family to do fun things can be bumped up to the top motivation levels by personalizing the task. After you've explained why the box should be moved and the benefits that will result, tell the adolescent why you think s/he can do a good job of it.

As always, call on your own experience. How well do you do a job when you receive recognition for your skill and effort? Personalization is the essence of excellence. People who feel truly appreciated for their personal contributions will not only move boxes better than anyone ever moved boxes before and dust them off to boot, they'll be back looking for more boxes to move.

When you focus on strengths in yourself and others, you strike internal chords that reverberate far beyond where you happen to be standing at the time. The influence you create by focusing on individual strengths has far-reaching and long-lasting effects. Peter F. Drucker told us that focusing on strengths places a demand on performance. I say high-performance people live on their strengths and therefore create a constant environment of excellence.

Level 4 (highest): Self-motivation

The only way to top the commitment of internalization is to have the motivation originate and emanate from inside of you. If the adolescent decides to straighten out the garage for some reason all his or her own, you can bet s/he will do the best job possible. The more you subscribe to the *high-performance process,* the more initiative you're bound to see emerge from your natural talents, knowledge, and experience.

If you're responsible for the performance of others as well as yourself, the same principles apply. The highest level of motivation will always result from self-initiative. Encouraging self-initiative takes skill as a leader, but it's well worth the effort. Once I learned from my sales mentor that my labors were tied directly to my lifestyle, my efforts started coming from within instead of needing to be associated with outside rewards.

Mental moods

Each of the four levels of motivation has an accompanying *mental mood.* Similar to the merry-go-round of *self-talk, self-image,* and *productivity,* your state of mind is a primary determinant in your level of motivation. At the same time, your level of motivation will fuel your state of mind. Your *mental mood* and your level of motivation dance together so closely that it's difficult to determine which one is leading.

Level 1 mental mood: Despair

When you're operating at the compliance level of motivation, you quickly begin to feel the frustration and futility of repeating yesterday over and over again. You tend to feel helpless or powerless. The resulting emotion is *despair.* The desperation you feel clouds any vision you might have of breaking the cycle, getting out of your rut and changing your life.

Without vision, there can be no goals. It's impossible to move up to the *goal identification* level without visualizing desired rewards. So your desperation tends to become a self-fulfilling prophecy. People who struggle in level one are aware of their despair, but they rarely have the vision to see any way out of it.

Level 2 mental mood: Reason

When you identify with a goal, it's possible to consider your desired rewards in realistic terms. Attaining what you want becomes more believable and justifiable. Applying yourself toward a goal makes sense when you identify with the anticipated outcome. At level two the process of goal attainment becomes more logical and easier to follow.

Your resistance to doing something will naturally diminish if the task makes sense to you. How reluctant would you be to do something if you had no idea what would happen as a result of your effort? If you don't have any reason to expect a profitable outcome for someone, even if that someone is not you, it's not likely that you'll be able to function at the second motivation level. Unless your mind can *reason* with the task, your mental involvement can't be expected to exceed unthinking compliance.

Level 3 mental mood: Intuition

At the commitment level of motivation, your logical mind gives way to the subconscious. When you've truly internalized a goal, the goal becomes part of you and you become part of the goal. You become so familiar with the desired rewards that attaining them seems like second nature to you. When a problem pops up, you correct it as if by instinct.

Other people observing you might comment that you seem to know just what to do without thinking. You're always thinking of course, but when you reach the intuitive stage, much of your mental processing goes on autopilot. When you're focused on an internalized goal, you can handle a much bigger load than you can at level one or two. With much of your thinking on autopilot, your mind is free to be more aggressive.

The subconscious engages when you've committed your talents, knowledge and experience. In other words, when your strengths are brought to bear on a task, every dimension of your personality becomes involved. When you observe someone who seems to be working intuitively, you can bet your bottom dollar that they're at the commitment level of motivation.

Level 4 mental mood: Self-confidence

When the impulse for action comes from within you, it is the product of your self-confidence. Doing something that comes from your heart means maximum inspiration. There's no need to convince yourself of the goal's merits or identify with the goal when your motivation is truly instinctive. You can't operate out of a more confident emotional position than to be self-motivated.

Befriending an unpopular fellow

When I first got into sales, just out of the Air Force, there was a guy in the office that nobody liked. There probably wasn't a single soul in that office who didn't pull me aside as a newcomer and say, "Stay away from that guy." When I asked why, I was told that he hated all other salespeople, but especially *new* salespeople. As I was warned about this fellow again and again, I couldn't help but keep an eye on him and my curiosity grew.

It seemed strange to me that this much-maligned salesperson was also the one with the most trophies, plaques and awards for top sales performance. Something didn't quite add up. So I made it my mission to get to know this guy and solve the mystery. I found out that even though professional jealousy cost him popularity in the office, he was popular with his *customers*.

I learned more from that guy than from anyone else in the organization. One day the two of us went out to prospect for new home listings. I should say that he convinced me to join him as he went out to prospect. As usual I was too busy planning to launch my plan into action. He helped me see the error in my ways. The first thing I felt was a slap on the back as I sat at my desk.

He said, "Let's go out and do some door-knocking, Danny." I replied that I had too much to do at the office to get out and solicit new business that day. As usual he asked me a question I couldn't answer, "What have you got to do in the office that's more important than drumming up new business." I wasn't sure how to answer him, but I knew that I didn't want to go out and bang on doors.

He got impatient with me. "What could you possibly do here at the office that's more important than to go out and find somebody who needs our help and is willing to pay well for it?" I had to admit there wasn't anything more important than that. He said, "Then let's go," and we launched out the door. Truthfully, he practically dragged me out to his big Cadillac.

He deposited me in the passenger seat and got in himself. As he started the engine, I noticed he was impeccably well dressed in an Italian silk suit with a white-on-white shirt. He looked the part of a successful person.

In stark contrast to his confident poise, I was slumped in the right front seat, an unwilling passenger. I felt like a hostage being driven away from the safety of my desk against my will. I liked planning as long as I never had to launch the plan. But here I was, too embarrassed to ask him to take me back. It was a good thing I was too meek to protest.

That man taught me one of the most important lessons of my life. As we drove I looked over at this man that I hated and loved at the same time and asked, *"Have you ever not wanted to go out and prospect?"* I wondered if he had ever, in his life, felt the way I was feeling at that moment. I had flown high-performance jet fighters to the very doorstep of disaster and yet I was afraid of talking to a few prospects.

He told me that he'd felt the same thing. He even went on to describe the queasy feeling I had in my stomach. He accurately recounted the whim-whams I felt all over my body. He could see the perspiration across my upper lip, but when he told me my tongue was stuck to the roof of my mouth I thought he was clairvoyant. Amazed, I asked, "How did you know that?"

He said, "I felt that way 20 minutes ago." I thought he was pulling my leg. That got my back up a little and I cautioned him not to mess with my head because I was on the verge of throwing in the towel and looking for another line of work. He reaffirmed that he had really faced trepidation similar to mine less than a half-hour earlier.

Seeing an opportunity, I said, "Let's go back to the office. Neither one of us has any business out here bothering these folks when we both feel the same way." He told me that he didn't feel fear anymore. It was hard for me to imagine that, once someone felt fear, they could get to a point of not feeling it. I asked him what his secret was; half believing it was still impossible.

That's when the lesson began. He asked me, "Danny, if I were to hand you a thousand dollars, what would you do with it?" I told him that I would pay some bills. "Wrong." He said it so fast it frightened me. I knew I hadn't given him the right answer. You know the feeling when you give the wrong answer and still have no clue as to the right answer. I took a stab and said, "Okay, if you gave me a thousand dollars I'd have some fun with it."

He wanted specifics. "What *exactly* would you do with it?" He persisted and I resisted. Finally, I told him that the Reno air races were coming up in a few months and I had always dreamed of going. I'd been to Reno before and loved it, but never attended the air races. He said that sounded good and asked me for some details about the weekend event.

I proceeded to tell him all about what I had read and learned about the three separate classes of swift and powerful planes. For anyone with any flying blood in them at all, watching those planes zoom past the crowd at full throttle, 40 feet off the ground, was sup- posed to send chills up your spine. I said, "That's what I would do with that $1,000."

He wasn't through with me yet. He asked where my wife and I would stay. He asked me to describe my favorite Reno restaurant. My descriptions were becoming incfeasingly detailed and exciting. A public relations/advertising firm couldn't have described a more incredibly delectable scene, right down to the steak dinner with twice-baked potato and homemade bread.

Still a little slow at the switch. I finished telling him how I would spend the money and then said, "Why do you ask? .... Why don't you figure up your side of the commission when we get a new listing today and sell the house?" In those days, it was $1,000. He knew what he was working for that day. I was going out to see if I could get lucky. He was going out with a purpose.

Then, he let me have it. "You were willing to forfeit your dream trip to Reno just so you could sit at the office and push papers around today then go home to tell your wife and kids how hard you worked at the office all day." I thought for a minute and said, "Would you drive a little faster?" When we hit that neighborhood, I was out of the car before he rolled to a stop.

I hit the ground running. Knocking on door after door, we stayed at it. An hour later I hopped back into his car with a big smile on my face and a listing appointment for that evening. We got the listing, sold the house and I went to the Reno air races for the first of 11 years in a row. The lesson I learned that day made my career the success that it was more than anything I learned in the corporate training materials.

Strangely, when he got back in the car that day, he had a grim look on his face. I was grinning from ear to ear and he was glaring at me. I asked him what was wrong. After all we had just set a listing appointment (and got two more leads that we later turned into listings and sales). From the look on his face I began to think that maybe the folks in the office were right about him.

In the aftermath of our successful prospecting that afternoon, he solemnly said, "I'm going to tell you something and don't ever forget it. Never work hard to pay bills. Work hard to have fun with the money. Otherwise, you won't have enough to do either one." I realized at that moment that I had been working hard to pay bills with the money. He was right. I didn't have enough to pay all my bills or have fun with the money.

The two things I despised the most, paying bills and knocking on doors, went hand in hand. I had no idea that I was operating at the lowest level of motivation and felt desperate. I had to do something I didn't like in order to do something else I didn't like. What a life! My sales mentor walked me right up the motivation ladder that day, from compliance to goal identification to commitment, from despair to reason to intuition.

Since that day, I've never worked to pay bills and my life has been filled with fun. Sure, I've had struggles along the way, but from the plains of Africa to the glaciers of Alaska, my wife and I have experienced adventure after adventure, filling our years with the most fascinating people and exotic places. The entire nature of work changes when you operate on the commitment level of motivation. Launching a plan into action at any other motivation level will compromise the outcome.

In a nutshell, the lesson I learned from my mentor, Jim Raco, in the sales business, was that as the "want" gets stronger, the "how" gets easier.

Laziness

When launching your plan into action, it's important not to forget about that old, insidious enemy, *procrastination*. Although procrastination can rear its ugly head at any stage of the *high-performance process,* it's most likely to appear when you put your thoughts into action. Risks are greater at the action stage because actions commit you more than words.

For that reason, you seldom procrastinate when talking. However, all sorts of things will creep up out of nowhere to keep you from acting. Of course these impediments to action usually come from within or are at least sanctioned by your own unconscious mind. Genuine roadblocks to your productivity that pop into your path are not part of a procrastination conspiracy.

In case you sometimes feel as if you're wasting a lot of time on a mediocre career, laziness is not a cause of reduced productivity, but a *symptom* of it. There are some people who are so genuinely lazy they don't know what to do when a holiday comes along. You know the kind who are born tired and then have a relapse. The type who don't want to work between meals.

However, the real reason we all tend to procrastinate can be broken down into three parts:

1. The inner fear of making a mistake.
2. Reluctance to shoulder an obligation.
3. The desire to avoid criticism.

Mistakes

Somewhere in our childhood, each of us learned that mistakes get frowns while victories get smiles of approval. Reacclimating ourselves as adults to believe that mistakes are not terrible, but in fact represent honest efforts and lessons learned is difficult but oh, so important to the *high-performance process*. If you go through life trying to avoid frowns, you'll never try anything. If you never try anything, the only big mistake you'll make will be not to try anything.

It sounds a little weird, but most high-performance people I've known in my life seem to seek out situations that have a high risk and a high probability for mistakes. That's where the prize is usually hidden. If the prize were laying in the middle of the street for everyone to reach down and pick up, everybody would be rich and/or successful.

Obligations

The high-performance people I know are quick to shoulder obligations as long as the obligation is necessary for the attainment of a worthwhile goal. High-performance people have no desire to shoulder the problems of the world. Just heaping responsibility upon yourself for no reason doesn't make sense. Yet some people feel guilty unless they're absolutely buried under more responsibility than they can possibly deal with.

Making a commitment means to accept responsibility for the outcome. It makes sense that someone who is afraid of making a mistake doesn't want to be held responsible for any sort of obligation. If you're the one responsible, you're the one who gets frowned at when things don't work out correctly. As long as you can avoid obligations, you can avoid mistakes. As long as you can avoid mistakes, you won't be criticized.

Critisism

Nobody likes to be criticized. The frown that we worked so hard to avoid as children can take on harsher and more pungent characteristics in adult life. Unfortunately, many of the firms I consult with owe a great deal of their productivity problems to an atmosphere of criticism. It takes a rare individual to plow ahead and take risks in a critical environment.

Nevertheless, high-performance people know that risking mistakes for the sake of breaking new and productive ground is well worth the potential penalty in criticism. If the great inventors and artists whose work has enhanced the quality of our lives over the centuries had allowed themselves to be stifled by criticism, our lives would be much poorer for it.

Criticism is a fact of life, like death and taxes. It's unfortunate that it seldom, if ever, helps anybody do anything better. But there it is, waiting for you around every bend. You can even watch low achievers and productivity saboteurs at meetings rubbing their hands together when others accept high-risk assignments.

Like vultures circling above a dying person in the desert, these buzzards of the business world hope others will make mistakes so that they can swoop down and pick the poor soul's bones clean. The desire to avoid having your bones picked clean is natural. To high-performance people, the desire to attain the rewards available only to risk-takers is stronger.

High-performance people know that criticism is not likely to come from the mouths of enlightened people. Part of the valuable respect for others that I described in the Overview means being a problem-solver rather than a people-basher. If you're willing to take risks for the sake of personal high-performance and excellence, you must be willing to take the heat.

It's somewhat comforting to know that only people who are not willing to take risks criticize others. Those who have experienced the slings and arrows of trying, failing, and trying again aren't prone to criticizing the courageous endeavors of other risk-takers. Noting who around you is quick to criticize and who is quick to encourage is a fast way to separate low achievers from high-performance people. High-performance people never allow laziness to take root in the fertile soil of procrastination.

A realistic look at fear

When you start talking about transforming thoughts and words into action, fear enters the picture. Fear is the driving force behind your old enemy procrastination. If you can successfully deal with fear, you can successfully deal with procrastination. Since fear is an inescapable part of life, it's best to do what Glenn Ford recommended and intentionally do the things that you're afraid of, thus keeping fear from taking charge of your life.

Some people have suggested to me that fear can be a positive influence in life and that my crusade against it is overstated. While I agree that fear is natural and it's always best to admit its presence and not deny it, I find little positive about fear. Even though it's good to pay attention to emotions because they're constantly telling you things about yourself that you might not otherwise be aware of, letting emotions govern your behavior is wrong.

Ask yourself how many good things fear has done for you. The answer is not very many. Fear influences your life to be sure, but the greater the influence fear plays in your life, the more it costs you in personal performance. The mental and physical exhaustion from battling fear alone can be overwhelming. Other than informing you how a situation affects you emotionally, fear has no other value.

Ask yourself if self-confidence does more for you than fear and the answer will be yes. Your self-confidence does far more to promote positive results in your life than fear ever will. How self-confident your self-image is determines how productive you are. Following the self-talk merry-go-round, your self-image is determined by your internal dialogue.

That leads to the next question. Which voice am I listening to right now, fear or self-confidence? The answer to that question is critical to your personal performance. As you think about what you're going to do next, both fear and self-confidence will have something to say about it. Which is speaking louder? Which are you going to listen to?

Usually, fear speaks with a louder voice than self-confidence. That's because fear has become a habit. Listening to self-confidence can become a habit too, if you work at it hard enough. Fear seems to come by its loud voice naturally. Self-confidence can only be amplified through your conscious effort. Self-confidence can be given a representative voice in your "self-talk, and your self-image and productivity will be much the better for it.

4 commitments for launching your plan

1. Honesty.
2. Courage.
3. Determination.
4. Conviction.

Honesty with yourself means taking initiative to look at things realistically. All the best-laid plans in the world aren't going to make me a player on a National Basketball Association team. I'm older now than I was when I started this book and I haven't grown an inch. You must be honest about what you're capable of and what you're willing to invest of yourself in the *high-performance process*.

It takes *courage* to set goals realistically high. Just because you can't do everything your heart can dream of doesn't mean you shouldn't try anything. Goals need to be realistic. But, if goals are to move you to a higher level of living, your targets need to be increasingly higher. That takes courage because the higher you reach, the farther you have to fall. Courage is more than a buzzword when it comes to launching a plan into action.

Determination to put the plan into action is fueled by desire. Because motivation is a by-product of desire, all three, *determination, motivation,* and *desire,* work in concert with one another to transform thoughts and words into action. Determination must be more than grim resolve and willpower.

There may be times when you need to give a push, However, identifying your true desires and level of motivation will have the effect of drawing the plan into motion rather than forcing it like the square peg through the round hole. Committing yourself to determination means committing yourself to giving: the plan a push if necessary.

Conviction that goals can be reached means believing that success is attainable. Your firm belief that your desired rewards are within reach is essential to your success. Without that belief, you won't have the resolve to keep investing when the going gets rough. There will be times when you begin to doubt and consider giving up on the plan.

It's in those moments that the strength of your conviction will either mean the salvation or abandonment of your actions. The stronger your conviction, the more likely you will be to deal in terms of *when* rather than *if*. Without a strong belief that your goals are attainable, you'll be prone to say, "If I go ahead and do such and such..." all the while straddling the fence in case the whole thing turns sour. A strong conviction sounds more like, "When I do such and such..."

The difference between thinking in *if* terms and *when* terms is the difference between *trying* and *intending* to do something. I know that many of us say that we intend to do something and then never do. The reason I mention a difference here is to illustrate how action varies from words. Look back on something you've done recently and ask yourself if you intended to do it or just whimsically gave it a try.

Sometimes we surprise ourselves and do worthwhile things without really trying. But it's never a way of life. If someone says to you, "I'll try and call this week" or "I'll try to squeeze you in for lunch," I doubt if you would clear your calendar in anticipation. Instead, if that person said, "I intend to call you Monday because we're going to have lunch before Friday," you'd get out your pencil and planner and ask, "What day looks good for you?"

Learn to talk to yourself in definitive action terms. Make *honesty, courage, determination,* and *conviction* part of your daffy language of higher productivity. When you break into the self-talk merry-go-round at the self-talk phase, those are the types of terms you want to add to your internal vocabulary. It doesn't do you any good to speak profoundly to others if you're not speaking profoundly to yourself.

> *"I'll take adventure before security, freedom before*
> *popularity and conviction before influence."*
> —Charles Lindbergh

That quotation is attributed to Charles Lindbergh by my friend, Jim Newton, who knew Lindbergh personally. Nobody can question the courage of the first man to cross the Atlantic in an airplane. When Jim was at the Smithsonian for the filming of a television documentary on Lindbergh, he turned to astronaut Neil Armstrong, who was also part of the film, and asked if he would have attempted the solo transatlantic flight.

Jim was a little surprised to hear one of America's greatest space heroes say no. Armstrong went on to explain that his mission to the moon was heavily researched, funded, and planned by teams of scientists who collectively knew about everything there was to know about space travel. The astronaut then pointed out that, while his Apollo mission had a supporting cast of a million, Lindbergh flew alone with no radio, no radar, no lights, no high-tech amenities. It was just one man up there, alone at the controls of a flying gasoline tank.

How do you spell relief?

Some people keep a little energy or effort in reserve as a bromide for their anticipated failures. When these folks try something new, they're so confident in their own failure that they give it less than they've got. Holding something back is a way of preserving an out more than a way to preserve energy. If their attempt falls short, they can always tell associates, friends, and family that they didn't give it their best shot. The implication is that their best shot would have assuredly succeeded.

Not every adventure you and I embark upon has the history-making potential of what Charles Lindbergh accomplished. However, whenever you or I break new ground in our lives and go places and do things we've never done before, the same principles apply. We need to call upon our own *honesty, courage, determination,* and *conviction.*

Life, where you are, doing whatever you do, must be played by the same rules if you're going to reap the rewards of the *high-performance process.* Lindbergh is a good example of how critical it is to launch your plan into action. Had his plans to cross the Atlantic Ocean in a single-engine airplane remained plans, it would have been up to someone else to accomplish the feat.

There's no doubt many people dreamed of and planned to cross the Atlantic just as Lindbergh did. The difference between Charles Lindbergh being heralded as the world's greatest aviator and the other would-be Atlantic-crossers was the fact that he, quite literally, launched his plan (and his plane) into action.

For some reason, many people would rather be able to make that excuse than to say that they gave it everything they had and it didn't fly. Contrary to popular opinion, the latter attitude of confession leads to success nine times out of 10, while the former attitude leads to success one time out of 10. It's not a matter of statistical probability as much as it is one of common sense. If somebody's trying with all they've got, it's perfectly natural to assume they will succeed more than someone who's not giving their all.

If you're going to fall, fall *toward your goal.* Big effort will beat small effort over time. Ask any athletic coach or player if withholding talent, knowledge and experience will lead to a starting spot on the team or cheers from the fans. Falling down or not falling down doesn't make you a hero. It's how and how often you get up and dust yourself off that brings the crowd to its feet.

When to expect results after a change of habit

When a group of people tries a new behavior day after day, approximately 20 percent of them will show tangible results within 30 days. The remainder usually meets expectations within 90 to 120 days if they keep at it. Do you have the patience to develop a new habit? The key is sticking to it. Successfully launching a plan into action requires *patience* and *persistence.*

Your forward motion will be faster at some times and slower at other times. The most important factor is your direction. As long as you're moving forward, you're sticking to your plan. Every moment you spend moving forward, you're adopting new and positive habits. That's what launching your plan means in behavioral terms—changing behavior for the better.

If life is to be an adventure, you must move forward. If you're a growing person, your largest adventures are ahead of you, not in your past. Monitor your motivation and mental moods to see if you need to move yourself up a notch. Deal realistically with fear and procrastination. Most of all, act. High-performance people know that *actions,* and not mere words, are what increases personal performance and improve the quality of your life. Real change comes from *doing.*

If you think there's no real need to launch your plan into action, consider what humorist George Ade said:

"Anyone can win, provided there's no second entry."

Step Five

Problem-solving: Expecting the Unexpected

"If a problem has no solution, it is not a problem but a fact of life like any other. If a problem has a solution, it is not a problem either. The problem is the strength of will and determination to adopt the solution."

—Richard Needham

When inventor Thomas Edison first tried to record the human voice on a piece of tin foil with a crude device he had assembled in his research lab, it worked. According to biographer Jim Newton, a personal friend of Edison's for many years, the inventor never trusted his voice-recording invention for the simple reason that it worked the first time he tried it.

Of the thousands of inventions Edison brought into our world, he fully expected to fail numerous times before he made any progress. He was a visionary who anticipated a difficult process every time. In other words, Edison knew that problems were part of life—and especially part of the creative process. If a great inventor like Edison could accept that, can it be that hard for us to learn?

Once, in his laboratory, Edison tried an experiment for the thousandth time. It failed. According to Newton, Edison turned to the researcher next to him and said, "We're making real progress. We now know 1,000 ways it can't be done." That's not only a positive attitude that all of us should strive to emulate, but also a great testament to learning.

"Fate seems to work with dice rather than a T square."
                                              —George Ade

Experience is another word for mistakes. Edison credited himself with failing more often than anyone else on Earth. Of course, he was trying *more new things* more often than anyone else on Earth. That's why he believed so strongly that the answer is always out there if only you work to find it. Experience is not only the best teacher in the world, but the most expensive. Once an answer is found, though, improvement and refinement come quickly.

Edison, best known for inventing the light bulb, had to patent more than 300 other inventions before he could install electricity in the Lower East Side of New York City. Before he could put the light bulb to practical use, he had to invent electrical wiring, meters, switches, and so on. The birth of a new idea might come slowly, but growing up is fast.

Even Alexander Graham Bell, who invented the telephone, couldn't put his revolutionary invention into application until Edison invented the carbon transmitter that allowed communities to finally enjoy the miracle of electronic communications. Bell's telephone was a great discovery, but its signal was too weak to be put to general use. The telephone, as great a discovery as it was, raised even greater and more profound problems by its very existence. Edison was instrumental in solving the problems posed by Bell's progress.

What Edison possessed in creative skills, he lacked in negotiating skills. Jim Newton recounts the story about Edison's invention of the carbon transmitter for the telephone. When the organization developing the telephone asked how much he wanted for inventing the new device, Edison thought of a price range in his head. It was $3,000 to $5,000 (a great deal of money in those days).

Not sure of himself as a negotiator, Edison replied, "What will you give me for it?" He was offered $25,000, which he promptly accepted. Afterwards, he told the men representing the early telephone company that he had a much lower figure in mind and, if they had held out, they could have got the transmitter for $5,000. They replied that, if Edison had held out, they were prepared to give him $50,000.

(Perhaps Edison's later invention of the motion picture camera was indirectly responsible for the evolution of the Hollywood agent.)

Today, we can't turn on an electrical appliance, launch a rocket into space, listen to a recording or see a movie without owing something to Thomas Edison. He had made 1,000 short films before the first film was ever shot in Hollywood.

Virtually everything worth having in life comes with some problems attached. Your progress and personal growth will never come without the need to resolve problems along the way.

Old you meets new you: shadow vs. light

As you discover and develop your potential, the new problems encountered are nothing more than the expanding shadow of your personal growth. The new you can solve problems that the old you couldn't. Once you successfully unleash your talents, knowledge and experience, you're essentially a new person. Realistically, you're more of who you always had the potential to be rather than a new creation.

Leonardo da Vinci said, "Shadows do not exist without their opposite light." Robert H. Schuller said, "If you're seeing only shadows, you're looking in the wrong direction." When I began my career as a lecturer and consultant, I saw many problems. I was worried about who was going to pick me up at the airport in the cities where I was scheduled to speak. How was I going to get around? Who was going to make sure I had the right hotel and all of the equipment I needed to make my presentation?

There were shadows everywhere. Then it occurred to me that I needed to book an engagement before any of my imagined problems would even apply. As my speaking career grew and prospered, I grew and prospered as a human being. Accordingly, I faced many problems along the way. That was the ever-expanding shadow of my personal growth. My real growth began as soon as I turned and looked toward the light and stopped focusing on the shadows.

As far as the way you handle your life, you might as well be a new person. If problems have eyes, they won't recognize you as a high-performance person, after knowing your old self. As you approach problems more aggressively, they'll appear far less intimidating. If you've delayed taking on an important task because you're hesitant to confront the inescapable problems that are bound to arise, you have allowed yourself to get seized by fear—you've become problem-phobic.

Preparation for problem-solving

Before I describe the concise problem-solving process, it's important for you to know how to prepare yourself and keep yourself prepared for problem-solving, from beginning to end. The steps in the problem-solving process seem simple and easy to execute. Indeed they will be more manageable if you use this preparation process to make sure your head's on right when you take on inevitable problems.

1. Stay calm and keep the problem in perspective.

It's easy to say that in a noncrisis atmosphere. Remembering to tell yourself to stay calm in a crisis will be more difficult. High-performance people know that those two key words, "stay calm," can make all the difference in the world when it comes to defeating a problem or allowing the problem to defeat you. All of your problem-solving skills become useless the moment you lose control.

When a problem pops up, whether it's a surprise or not, staying calm needs to be your *first* priority. Memorizing those two words is a good place to start. Have them so ingrained in your mind that when other people are saying, "Holy cow! What am I going to do?" You'll be saying, "Stay calm." If that's your knee-jerk reaction to a surprise problem, you'll be establishing an atmosphere for problem-solving while others are still trying to decide whether to run and hide.

2. Be aware of your self-confidence.

> *"You can tell the character of the person by*
> *the choices made under pressure."*
>
> —Winston Churchill

The late Dr. Norman Vincent Peale said, "You're only as big as the problem that stops you." Think about the last time a problem stopped you in your tracks and you decided to abandon your efforts. Can you recall how pumped up you were initially about reaching that goal and collecting your desired rewards? What happened? Did you change your mind?

You probably didn't change your mind about how valuable your goal was. Instead, a problem probably came up that made the desired rewards look less desirable than the amount of effort required to solve the problem. That's not a change of perspective as far as the goal is concerned. It's more likely to be a distortion created by your own problem-phobia.

In hindsight, I doubt if you can find many instances in your life when abandoning the goal was a suitable trade-off compared to any threat the problem might have presented. How much further along in your career would you be if you had gone ahead and faced that problem and then, having overcome it, continued on your charted course?

Knowing that you have talent, knowledge, and experience (in this case especially experience), you must ask the question that calls out your self-confidence for inspection. Right after you say to yourself, "Stay calm," ask yourself, "Is this problem more than I can handle?" In the past, have you ever solved problems that are similar or even larger? Probably.

What's the worst that can happen if you forge ahead? Will somebody yell at you? Will it cost you a great deal of money? Will it cost you your job? Worst of all, will people expect more of you in the future if you succeed? That last one stops more folks than any of the other questions. If you have the confidence that you can overcome the problem, then get started. If you don't feel you have the confidence, get started anyway. Every step you take toward solving the problem will increase your confidence.

3. De-confuse the problem. Define it and break it down to its component parts on paper.

A big, intimidating challenge is really just a collection of smaller, less-intimidating challenges. When a problem hits, it's natural to experience confusion. Problems don't present themselves in neat, easy-to-understand packages. It's not unusual to feel disoriented. Just because you can see the front end of a problem doesn't mean you can see the back end or even the middle. How do you know that's the front end you're looking at anyway?

You've told yourself to *stay calm* and you've decided that there's enough self-confidence in your tank to take this thing on. Now calmly begin dismantling the problem before it dismantles you. Writing things on paper engages the linear lobe of your brain where logic is the order of the day. Trying to sort things out in your head means you will be using, at least partially, the spatial lobe of your brain where your imagination can run wild.

Your right brain will come into play soon enough. There's nothing like imagination to feed the creativity you need to solve the problem. First, you have to know what it is you're trying to solve. As logic and reason kick in from your linear/logical brain lobe, you will begin to feel an increasing sense of control. A model will begin to emerge from your list of the problem's component parts.

When the problem has been sketched out, it will no longer seem confusing or intimidating. In fact, you're now setting the stage for the fun part of problem-solving. Because of the focus that problems require, they can contribute beneficial refinement to your goal-attainment process. Problems often act as stones that wear away the rough edges of your plan rather than as roadblocks.

4. Use creativity, personal experience and/or the experience of others to solve the puzzle from start to finish, from finish to start, or begin in the middle.

Out of conflict comes creativity. You've stayed calm, called out your self-confidence, and sketched out a profile of the problem on paper. Now you've got the problem right where you want it. The problem now becomes a vehicle to bring out all that's best in you. Moreover, you can have fun in the process. Consider the problem as a unique challenge that your talents and abilities will ultimately resolve, possibly with the help of solutions suggested by others.

Orison Swett Marden, a great thinker and author chronicled the lives of great people who left their marks on the world. The people he studied and wrote about didn't become well-known because they didn't have problems. Great people become known for the way they managed to deal with problems—and even turned problems into opportunities.

Marden was the original founder of *Success* magazine and continually urged his readers to "ride on the shoulders of giants." His contention, and the basis for the early magazine, was that time you spend covering the same territory that someone else has covered is time wasted. He might have even been the one who coined the phrase about reinventing the wheel.

Your personal knowledge and experience are very important, but should be used as a supplement to what you can learn from the experience of others. Once again, reading, attending seminars and studying audio and video materials can enrich your talents and save you tremendous time as you go about the business of problem-solving. You can start at the public library.

If you're unclear about where to start on a problem, try visualizing the final solution and work backward from there. If you know where you want to go or can picture the desired outcome, it becomes easier to backtrack and apply some reverse engineering to build the bridge you need. Sometimes the view is clearer from some point other than the front end.

You might as well have fun solving your problems. That's where much of your time's going to be spent. Frank A. Clark said, "The next best thing to solving a problem is finding some humor in it." I say that finding humor in the problem-solving process will speed up the solutions. It's not necessarily true that, if you can smile when things go wrong, it's because you've got someone else in mind to blame. On the other hand, if someone says, "This is as bad as it can get," don't count on it.

5. Use relentless, dogged determination until the solution is in action.

Problem-solving, like planning, doesn't begin to benefit anyone until ideas are implemented. You need a Ph.D. in *stickology*. Remember how I like to shake up boardrooms full of top executives by having them review their meeting notes from past problem-solving sessions? The ugly truth I bring them face-to-face with is their own lack of action. They talk about their problems, even come up with good solutions, but seldom do they boldly put those solutions into action.

Solutions really aren't solutions until they're in action. Up to that point, they're just thoughts and talk. One of the reasons that solutions aren't implemented is because they're too simple. For some reason people tend to believe that a solution has to be complex and profound to be useful. Thomas Edison himself would argue that solutions don't have to be fancy to be good solutions.

The problem-solving process

Against the backdrop of your mental preparation for problem-solving, the following steps give you a practical blueprint for taking on any problem that pops up as you carry out your plan:

1. *Identify the problem.* How will you know where you're going if you don't first figure out where you are? Being clear about what the problem *is* and what the problem *is not* will save you time and energy as you seek solutions.

    For example, it's often thought that people are problems and roadblocks when it's a misunderstanding or communication disruption. The people don't need to be fixed; the communication does. Separating people from problems is almost always a good first step.

2. *Gather all relevant information.* It's imperative that you know as much about the problem as possible. By this I'm not suggesting that you spend an inordinate amount of time on negative issues. The point is to understand the nature of what you're up against.

    If you're not sure if your problem is a result of implementation or planning, where are you going to begin? The more information you have, the more quickly you'll be able to diagnose what you're up against.

3. *List all possible solutions.* This one helps build self-confidence right off the bat. As your list of possible solutions grows, the problem becomes less menacing. When

you've got your mind engaged in problem-solving, it's neither fair nor smart to try to keep lists in your head.

By having a list of all possible solutions nearby, you can quickly scan to see if what you're doing could be enhanced by incorporating a component of another solution. When the solution you're trying doesn't bear fruit, a list will speed you on to the next try.

4. *Test possible solutions.* In prioritizing the list of solutions you come up with, it may be difficult to determine with any certainty which solutions are the most promising. In that case, testing solutions will help make that determination.

Again, I urge you not to spend needless time testing every solution that comes to mind. Instead, only test those that hold the most promise and can't be clearly eliminated by pondering. Testing or trial runs will help you correctly prioritize the top few solutions on your list.

5. *Select the best solution.* Sounds easy, doesn't it? You'll be glad you took time to test your top choices when it comes time to throw all of your energy and effort behind the best possible solution. You want to be as sure as you can be, but even when you've still got some doubt about which solution is absolutely best, you will have to make a choice. Whatever solution you choose, make sure you go with it 100 percent.

6. *Get the solution into action.* I might sound like a broken record on this point but it's the most important. Just like launching your plan was the key step in the *high-performance process,* implementing your solution is the key step in the problem-solving process.

People are hesitant to implement solutions in the problem-solving process for many of the same reasons they hesitate when launching their plans. There is an element of risk. Go back and dig into some of the courage, determination, and conviction I talked about in step five and do it.

The High- Performance
Communication System

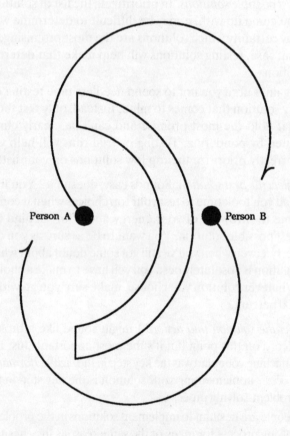

Person A   Person B

Figure 5.1

The art of persuasion

Sometimes your problem is convincing others to adopt your point of view. The *high-performance communication system* (see Fig. 5.1) is based on a process that former Disney executive Mike Vance explained to me many years ago. When adopting a new solution, you might have to "sell" others on the plan or possibly even a definition of the problem.

To overcome resistance, you must, first of all, accept that the other person might be looking at the same wall you are, but from the opposite side. A curved wall might be convex from your perspective, but concave from the opposite perspective. In the Figure 5.1 illustration, person A must take a trip around to view the wall from the perspective of person B.

Person A must ask as many questions as possible while standing in person B's position. Person A must list every possible objection person B might articulate based on his or her perspective. If, after examining things from all relevant sides, person A has not improved upon or come up with a better solution, it's time to talk.

Discussing a problem after you've taken the time to ingest what the other party might think based on his or her perspective puts you light years closer to arriving at a consensus. You won't be tempted to force your perspective on the other person once you've seen theirs. The whole dialogue will begin and proceed on common ground, which makes agreement much more likely.

Remember, a problem between two people is not solved until there is agreement. Just having a great solution in mind isn't enough. Effective communication is critical to the problem-solving process.

How much water will a light bulb hold?

Every year, Edison invited students from MIT and other top schools to assist and observe in his research laboratory. The renowned inventor gave the incoming students a problem to solve as a means of getting their heads on straight. Jim Newton tells the story of how Edison asked two MIT students to determine the weight of the water required to fill the bulb.

Working separately, the two ran exhaustive calculations and calibrations that would make any college professor proud. They came back to Edison with two different answers and everyone in the lab wondered how the old man was going to determine which was right. The first thing Edison did was ask for the bulb back. He then put it on the scale and weighed it. Next he removed the end of the bulb, filled it with water and weighed it again.

By subtracting the weight of the empty bulb from the weight of the bulb filled with water, he knew the weight of the water filling the bulb. The students were a bit embarrassed that he found his answer so simply and quickly. But, coming from an academic, and—shall I say *bureaucratic*—environment, they never considered his direct approach. Edison realized this and said to them, "There is your answer. Now forget everything they taught you at MIT. "

Edison also liked to say, "There's no extreme to which a [person] won't go to avoid the labor of thinking." When you're all wrapped up in finding a solution to a problem, you might think you're thinking. It's more likely that you're avoiding the clear thinking that will bring a simple and direct solution to mind. When the simple and direct solution hits, what excuse do you have for not taking action?

Harvey S. Firestone, another longtime friend of Jim Newton's, got successful enough to eventually need an engineering department. Nothing was as much fun after that for the entrepreneurial Firestone. As the story goes, the Firestone company developed a brake lining powder and the product development folks brought it, all neatly packaged, to Harvey.

The company founder asked if the package would withstand shipping. His employees looked at each other and decided to take the problem to engineering to determine if the packaging could withstand shipping. Firestone stopped them, took the package and shook it hard. It broke open, spilling the powder all over his office. He handed the package back to one of his people and said, "It won't withstand shipping."

Henry Ford was another character who could cut through the cackle and get to the corn. Jim Newton recalls an incident that involved Ford's engineering department and a no-nonsense boss. Henry ordered a design change on the fender of his early automobiles. He gave the design idea to engineering and then checked back about a week later.

The engineers told him that they needed a few more days and Ford checked in with them again. The company founder was again told that engineering needed a few more days. Ford went straight from engineering to the factory floor where the old fenders were still being stamped out. He ordered the stamping machines stopped and had the fender molds removed and placed in the middle of the floor.

He then had the biggest worker he could find take a sledgehammer and break each mold in the middle. The man who developed the assembly line brought his own plant to a dead stop in order to light a fire under his engineering department who had decided to make a career out of solving one design problem. The new fender design was not only completed but available online very quickly.

Problems due to error

We create some problems for ourselves. Any problem that's due to an error should only appear once. If the same problem appears again, the lesson of the first problem was never learned. Peter F. Drucker says, "A crisis must never be experienced for the second time." *Planning, judgment,* and *implementation,* in that order, should be your plan for troubleshooting a problem that's caused by your own efforts. If the problem you're faced with is due to an error, immediately check your planning to determine where and how you set yourself up for the problem.

Review your judgment. Perhaps it was your thinking that allowed the problem to occur. Everyone can always learn to make better judgments. I don't feel comfortable turning a project over to a person who thinks s/he knows it all. Someone who is always open to learning and improving his or her own judgment will do a better job by allowing for more possibilities.

Maybe your plan was fine and you didn't err in your judgment. It's possible that the solution was implemented improperly. Getting thoughts into action is important, but getting them into action *correctly* is even more important. If the problem is due to an error in implementation, you then know where to take corrective action.

Mary Lawrence, the problem-solver

After her near-fatal automobile accident, Mary Lawrence had many problems to deal with, any one of which would put a lesser person on public assistance. She was a great one for finding a practical, no-nonsense solution and putting it into action. One of her biggest problems was her lack of memory. The accident left her so impaired that she had a difficult time remembering how she began a sentence by the time she ended it.

That's why she spoke so deliberately on the telephone. She had to concentrate on every word. Passing her licensing exam was a result of endless hours of literally memorizing the codes and regulations. When it came to speaking with customers on the telephone and in person, she carried a small tape recorder. She repeated everything someone said to her on the phone about what they wanted in a home.

Mary didn't have shorthand skills and wasn't able to take notes that would make any sense to her after she hung up the telephone. By then all recollection of the call would be lost. She didn't break the law by recording someone over the telephone, instead she told them she was writing down the information. In reality, she was taping her end of the conversation, which she referred to over and over as she made her notes.

When she showed a house, Mary spoke into the recorder to store valuable information about her clients' needs and desires, explaining to the clients that she was keeping a detailed file on them back at the office—which she was. In virtually every case the clients were impressed that she would work so hard to keep tabs on what they wanted. Mary had problems and Mary found solutions. Most of all, Mary stayed in action. Today she's a millionaire property owner, proving that even the most difficult problems can be solved.

The not-so-helpful helper

I know a fellow who would give you the shirt off of his back if you needed it. He's truly one of the most unselfish people on the face of the earth. He told me about an experience he once had helping out a fellow traveler. It was a hot and humid summer day as my friend was driving between Chicago and Detroit. About an hour and a half west of Detroit, he was driving along in the air-conditioned comfort of his car when he spotted a man beside the road.

One glance told him that the man was hot and exhausted. The man's tie was loosened and his collar was open. There was a gasoline can sitting beside the man who had his thumb up in the air and an I-know-you're-not-going-to-stop-either look on his face. Dick, being the Good Samaritan that he is, pulled over. The man ran up to the car with newfound energy.

The man was exceedingly grateful and told my friend that he was beginning to believe no one was going to give him a ride. The gasoline can had no lid so they decided to wedge it between some suitcases in the trunk rather than risk spilling it in the car. With the gasoline can secured they were off. On the way, the poor traveler told my friend about how he had walked 20 miles in just over four hours to get to the gas station and spent almost another two hours trying to thumb a ride.

My friend told me later that he never felt more alive than when he was helping this stranger solve his problem. Apparently hundreds of cars had gone by and no one stopped. Now they were on their 20-mile journey back to where the man's car had run out of fuel. My friend pulled over and let the exceedingly grateful man out.

As my friend pulled away he was bursting with satisfaction at his good deed. He gave the man a salute in the rearview mirror and drove the remaining 90 miles to Detroit. As he opened his trunk to unload his luggage, *there sat the man's gasoline can.* True story. My friend still has nightmares about what that man must have felt as he realized my friend wasn't coming back.

The moral of this story is:

Don't forget the person you've dedicated yourself to help

or

Don't get so wrapped up in the excitement and satisfaction of problem solving that you forget to solve the problem.

Always remember the same adversity that causes some people to break causes others to break records. As Confucius said, "The gem cannot be polished without friction, nor [people] perfected without trials." Make problems a tool as you engineer your success. Problems won't go away. If they're not working for you, they're working against you.

Keeping Morale High

> *"Keep away from people who try to belittle your ambition. Small people always do that, but the really great people make you feel that you, too, can become great."*

—Mark Twain

Whenever you venture out and attempt the new and different, your personal morale will be tested. Through the planning and launching phases of the *high-performance process* your morale and motivation tend to peak with anticipation. As the problems arise and you reach the bleak midwinter of your process, your morale will come under assault.

As a high-performance person, you need to understand how your personal growth and increased productivity are tied to morale. If morale is not given sufficient consideration, you will unwittingly sabotage your efforts. Major stumbling blocks and other obstacles to your progress are obvious and are overcome with head-on confrontation or clever manipulation.

The erosion of your morale is something altogether different. Loss of morale is an insidious, creeping menace that will quietly eat at you like cancer. It sneaks up on you like termites eating away the floorboards in your house. You might not know that you have a morale problem until you fall into the basement one day. You'll probably sit there on the basement floor and scratch your head saying, "I think I have a morale problem." The fact is you had one long before you fell through the floor.

Don't wait until it's too late to deal with morale issues. By the time they become apparent, it might be too late to save the structure. Morale is an issue that requires attention every day.

A. M. Maslow, who documented the hierarchy of needs, also developed the *four levels of learning*. I've added a fifth level:

Level 1: Unconscious incompetence

Down in southern Illinois where I come from, *unconscious incompetence* would be described as messing something up without even knowing you're messing it up. Of course you're not happy once you begin to pay the penalty for what you've screwed up. It's only for the moment that you're doing it that ignorance is bliss.

Level 2: Conscious incompetence

When you become aware that you don't know what you're doing, you've graduated to Maslow's second level of learning. Operating on learning level two does not produce loads of self-confidence. People usually engage in activities they're not prepared for because they want the rewards anyway. Pride also encourages us not to admit when we're not sufficiently trained for something. In short, we don't want to look stupid.

At other times, knowing that you're operating outside of your expertise is helpful in not taking on tasks or assignments at which you might fail. You can use the awareness of your own incompetence as a guide to what you're prepared to do and what you're not prepared to do. At the same time, you don't want to restrict yourself from trying new things and growing simply because you're being called upon or challenged to do something new. Knowing your limitations will help you to handle your new endeavor more responsibly.

Level 3: Conscious competence

Conscious competence means you can do something correctly as long as you think about what you're doing. As a pilot, I'm sure that any of my passengers wanted me operating on level three. Any time you enter the operating room at the hospital, you'll want the surgeon and the attending staff to be operating at a conscious level of competence.

Operating at level three requires intense focus on your project. You have the training, the natural talent, the knowledge, and the experience to do something, but you can't apply those resources lightly. Level three can be the most exciting level in which to function. When you're keenly conscious of your skills, you tend to appreciate them more. It's not uncommon to feel proud when you're doing something well for the first time or doing something exceedingly well.

Do you remember the first time you drove an automobile on your own? You had studied and been taught about driving, but it felt very different to do it yourself. Your first driving experiences were no doubt emotionally stimulating and even exhilarating. Then came a time that you drove all the way across town, making numerous stops and turns.

Level 4: Unconscious competence

When you first parked your car, got out and began to walk away without thinking about what you had just done, you had crossed the line into level four, *unconscious competence.* Driving had become second nature to you. It no longer required intense focus nor produced a feeling of accomplishment.

You've probably experienced the same transition in a job. What might have begun as a stimulating challenge, with a rewarding sense of accomplishment, eventually became mundane. You might have changed jobs in the past because the job ceased to be a challenge. People tell me all the time that they want a change of scenery in their professional lives. They say that they need a new challenge to stimulate them.

I'm not recommending that you change career paths any time you become extremely competent at what you're doing. There are many ways to increase challenges within the scope of your present responsibilities. The first place to look is a part of your job you don't do particularly well. What are the things you *avoid doing* because they don't come as easily or effortlessly?

You can lead yourself right back through the emotionally invigorating *conscious competence stage* by developing a new skill or venturing into an area that has made you nervous in the past. That's why I added the fifth level of learning, *conscious of unconscious competence.* By being conscious of your unconscious competence, you are aware of your situation and can avoid its perils.

Level 5: Conscious of unconscious competence

You can put the spring back in your step by making efforts similar to the ones I just described to find new challenges and new responsibilities. I don't mean jump ship and replicate what you've done in one place in another place. That's not personal growth. Increasing personal productivity through the *high-performance process* always means you'll be conscious of emotionally stimulating efforts to push back your threshold of undeveloped strengths.

Becoming conscious of your unconscious competence brings you full-circle back to your personal moment of truth. If you're in a career position that has ceased to challenge you, the question becomes, "Do I want to stay here and grow or go somewhere else and do what I did here?" That's a more provocative question than it might seem at first blush.

If you stay and make what you're doing more challenging and fulfilling, you have no choice but to grow as a human being and increase your personal productivity. To move laterally to another position means that you can keep doing the same old stuff over and over. The only difference is the scenery. You've probably already found out that even new scenery becomes old over time.

Job hopping, career hopping, marriage hopping, and geography hopping all tend to seduce you for a short time and convince you that the future will be different. But that's seldom if ever the case. If you aren't growing as a person and pushing back your threshold of undeveloped strengths, you're bound to eventually stagnate anywhere you go.

Taking whatever challenges you the most about your job, and bringing that challenge into level three, the exciting time of *conscious competence,* will spice up your life wherever you are. It could be improving organization skills, communication skills, becoming more involved with others, taking on a new and dynamic assignment or any number of things.

How about just increasing your level of personal productivity? There's no one alive who has maxed-out his or her productivity potential. The more you learn, the more you become aware of how much you don't know. Consider the cliche, "A little knowledge is a dangerous thing." How many times have you seen the havoc wrought by someone who *thought* s/he knew a lot but didn't?

A little knowledge is not in and of itself dangerous. Someone operating well outside of his or her universe of competence can be exceedingly dangerous. The ideal level of operation remains level three, *conscious competence.* It's true that having skills and talents so ingrained that they become second nature will elevate your skill level. However, you still want to be keenly aware of what you're doing and be excited about it.

I'll use my surgeon simile again. If you came out from under you anesthesia for some reason right in the middle of an operation, would you rather hear your surgeon talking about his golf game the day before or how marvelously the operation is proceeding? Think about it. You might say you want a surgeon who is so skilled, s/he can successfully remove organs without thinking about it. On the other hand, you darn well want him or her thinking about it while s/he's doing it.

Unconscious competence is terrific as long as you are functioning in an energized state of *conscious competence.* If you're aware of your *unconscious competence* and still don't feel compelled to read, study, attend seminars or consult with a mentor, why not? Are you that content where you are? Have you become complacent? Maybe you've simply not been doing what you're doing long enough. Trust me, without investing in your personal growth, you're going to sink into a hypnotic rut.

Someone once said, "You don't grow old. You become old by not growing." Is that ever true! Haven't you noticed that the great artists, entertainers, scientists, authors, and thinkers all seem to be somehow timeless? They can be 80 or 90 years old and they're still as enchanted by new and innovative things as they ever were.

People like Thomas Edison, Bob Hope, Norman Vincent Peale, Mother Teresa, Grandma Moses, Norman Rockwell, and others are known for their longevity. Or are they really known for ongoing activity throughout their lives? Lots of people live to be 80, 90, or more than 100 years old. How come they're not all famous if the number of years you live is the only criteria?

As I mentioned earlier, whoever first said, "It's the amount of life in your years, not the number of years in your life that counts," had a valuable and timeless message for every man, woman and child who ever lived. Growing as a human being keeps your morale high. There's nothing else like it. If you wonder where the vigor of your youth has gone, it's fallen victim to stagnation. To get it back you must do what you did when you were young and invigorated—grow.

Feelings as habits change

You can see in Figure 6.1 the four progressive emotional levels that accompany the acquisition of new skills and the development of new strengths. Part of understanding the vital role of morale in your personal development is to accept that it's going to change as you change. For every improvement in your emotional state, there is a potential trap door you might fall through if you're not aware and vigilant.

Level 1: Guilt and shame

When you first try something, it's likely that you'll set yourself up for some disappointing results. Unrealistic expectations are common to new efforts. When I first entered the sales business right out of the Air Force I still had my gung-ho, fly boy confidence. I told the other

Feelings (and Trap Doors)
During Change of Habits

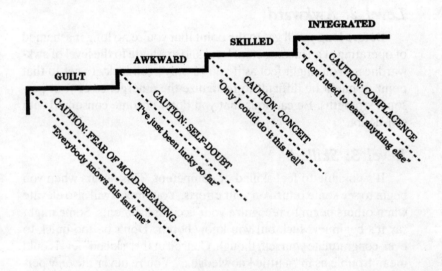

Figure 6.1

salespeople in my office that I didn't need to prospect for new business, I just sold off inventory.

Before long I was a more humble sales professional out prospecting. How did I feel? Guilty. You might say to yourself, *"Everybody knows this isn't really me doing this."* Unfortunately, it is you, and you don't feel very good about it. At this level you are very aware of your incompetence. Beware that you don't develop a fear of mold-breaking. Sometimes you have to break the mold if it's not productive or realistic.

Level 2: Awkward

Before long you'll get to the point that you're no longer ashamed of operating at an incompetent level and graduate to the level of awkwardness. You might feel as if you've only been lucky to get to that point. It might be difficult to recognize the emergence of your personal strengths. Be cautious that you don't become consumed with self-doubt.

Level 3: Skilled

It's possible to feel skilled or competent. This occurs when you begin to see some return on your efforts. Your mood will also elevate when others begin to recognize your accomplishments. Some might say it's beginners luck but you know better. Don't be too quick to over-congratulate yourself, though. Conceit at the "skilled" level could mean trouble as in "a little knowledge..." You're never the *only* person who can do well and other people don't appreciate being told that you are.

Level 4: Integrated

The change of habit or new behavior becomes part of how you go about your business. You feel the most confident at the integration level. What was once embarrassing, became awkward and then skilled, and is now a developed strength. Now it's part of you. It's second nature. You can comfortably rely on what you're now capable of doing.

Your self-confidence bolsters your morale. The only caution here is to not feel as if you can stop growing and be satisfied. You already know better than that, Part of keeping morale high is remembering where you came from and how much progress you've made. Knowing that, if you made the journey once, you'll be able to make it again, is a morale booster.

Survival training

I flew single-engine jet fighters over some of the most rugged mountain country in the United States, the Philippines, China, the South Pacific and points in between. The key term in the previous sentence is *"single-engine"* jet fighters. When your one and only engine decides to quit, you stand the chance of going from *king of the sky* to becoming an *unwanted guest in hostile territory* in a matter of moments. I wanted to be as prepared as possible.

I attended every survival school I could locate. Everything sounded good in the classroom because we always broke for lunch. But on a survival trek, alone in the wilderness, I once lost 18 pounds in seven days. Dirt and bark don't have a high calorie content. It's difficult to appreciate the amount and variety of food you take for granted until you spend a week away from it.

The classroom instructor for military survival training is always the same character—different people, but the same character. I swear they must go to Central Casting to find these guys. They're always craggy-faced, old, rugged, and gruff, with pants tucked into highly-polished boots and stripes from cuff to shoulder. They were the forerunners of today's motivational speakers.

The survival instructors got me so pumped up about the adventure of survival in the wilderness that I used to dream about one day punching out of my aircraft just to prove I could survive out there. These guys would pace back and forth in front of the class and point at us as they lectured:

"I'll tell you what's going to happen to you, Captain. One day you're going to be sitting up there in that multimillion dollar jet and it's going to have a serious case of the 'come-aparts' on you.

"Then you're going to decide to get out of there and the ejection seat will lift you out of any situation you determine is intolerable. That 35ram cannon shell under your seat will lift you 150 to 175 feet above the aircraft and you're going to parachute down somewhere in the wilderness.

"You'll be out in that wilderness for two, three, four days or more before we find you and, when we do find you, you'll be dead, graveyard dead, unless you..."

I decided to make a special note of whatever he was going to say next. I imagined that he might say something like, "...unless you parachute into a McDonalds restaurant, a cornfield or a high school reunion picnic." He didn't say any of those things. What he said caught me off guard. He said:

"You'll be dead unless you have a feeling of accomplishment on a daily basis."

"Huh ?" Just as I was all set to write down something about how to find food, the instructor takes a sharp turn and starts talking about *emotional health*. He was serious as he went on to explain that, unless you have a feeling of accomplishment on a daily basis, your deteriorating morale will kill you faster than the wilderness will.

15 steps for keeping morale high

I offer you yet another list to consolidate some of the many activities you can engage in to boost your morale and keep it high regardless of your circumstances. I do all of these things. Some may appeal to you more than others, but they all have value. If you gave it enough thought, you could assemble your own list of things that you do, even without thinking about them, that brighten your mood.

1. Lay out a new list of goals.

Doesn't that sound like a lot of fun? I didn't think so I've heaped a ton of goal-setting and morale-building thoughts on you in this book. You've been buried under this list and that list. Why would you want to make another?

Remember what the survival instructor said about feeling a sense of accomplishment on a daily basis. Laying out a new goal list on a regular basis, especially a list of goals for the next 24 hours, sets you up for accomplishing a few things. The fact that you *listed* your goals makes you all the more aware of their accomplishment.

Improving your situation on a daily basis gives you the *feeling of accomplishment* necessary to sustain life. You don't want someone to find you dead in your office. Dwelling on the past (over which you have no influence) and worrying about the future (over which you have no influence) will kill you, or at least make you wish you were dead.

Operating in the *conscious competence* of the moment, where you can influence your destiny, will produce the sense of hopefulness to sustain you.

2. Go for a walk.

A solo stroll in the park, on the beach, or in the mountains will have a rejuvenating effect on your psyche. Incidental pause and repose from your workload give your spirits a lift by momentarily lifting the load. When you have your nose to the grindstone, you're forcing all of your energies through a pretty narrow corridor. Giving your mind an opportunity to wander in wide open spaces, away from your principle place of business, will help restore morale.

3. Buy (and read) several books on various topics.

Even if you're not an avid reader, force yourself to read a book or two from time to time. Don't, however, force yourself to read only on topics of success or increasing your personal performance. Read fiction or whatever. The act of reading is what will exercise atrophied parts of your brain that otherwise might be ignored.

4. Get away for a weekend to a luxury hotel or spa.

Definitions of what's luxurious vary from person to person. The important factor here is to be pampered. If you're used to working and driving hard, why not let someone wait on you for a couple of days? Again, it breaks the routine, changes the focus and gives your emotional batteries an opportunity to recharge.

You may personally prefer a weekend camping in the mountains or by the seashore. If your weekend is an extension of the well-ordered, matter-of-fact way that you work, you're not gaining much. Avoid skipping weekend opportunities figuring you'll take one or two extended vacations per year. I have nothing against extended vacations, but once your batteries are dead, they're dead until you recharge them. That suggests to me that mini-vacations on a regular basis are important.

5. Get in better physical condition.

How you feel physically has a profound effect on how you feel emotionally. The reverse is also true. The higher your morale is, the better you will feel physically. Absenteeism in a high-morale environment is only a fraction of what it is in a low-morale environment. All of these suggestions are tips on pumping up your personal morale. Walk, swim and/or join a health club and exercise on a regular basis. Your peak physical conditioning is another way to feel a sense of accomplishment.

6. Buy something you've always wanted.

If you're the kind of person who shops incessantly as a way of soothing anxiety, this isn't a good suggestion for you. The point of buying something you've always wanted is to combine personal reward with personal effort. That way, planning for, saving for (if necessary) and purchasing something that's been on your wish list for a long time produces yet another feeling of accomplishment.

7. Invite interesting people over for dinner.

Author James Newton got to know Thomas Edison, Henry Ford, Dr. Alexis Carrel, Harvey Firestone, and Charles Lindbergh mostly by sharing meals and nonworking hours with them. Sharing relaxing, nonwork time with stimulating people, especially those who are not in the same field you are, is another way to open up parts of your brain that otherwise tend to stay locked up. Hearing other people's perspectives can't help but to widen yours.

8. Listen to good music.

Like reading a variety of books, music calls out certain brain functions that you probably don't exercise on a regular basis. It doesn't matter if you and your spouse or family agree on what "good" music is. You need to listen to something that pumps you up. If there are lyrics, sing along, preferably at the top of your lungs. Again, you're accessing parts of your brain that aren't given much exercise in your day-to-day affairs to elevate your mood.

Someone suggested to me that I listen to classical music to calm my mind. I had never listened to classical music before. Now I listen to classical music constantly. I even carry a portable cassette player with headphones when I travel. Taking your mind in a direction it wouldn't ordinarily go has an incredible calming and rejuvenating effect.

9. Organize your home and office.

When your home and office are cluttered, you feel as if you're out of control. Many people blame a sloppy office or home on being creative. I think that's an excuse for not taking control of their lives. Being in control, even of just your personal environment, means taking responsibility for it. I've already discussed why some folks avoid that. But ordering your personal environment is a sign of control and adds to your sense of accomplishment, thus propping up your personal mood.

10. Go see a funny movie or comedian.

In other words, *laugh*. There's nothing like laughter to remind you that life isn't to be taken too seriously. When you lose perspective, it's usually because you're giving too much consideration to something that would be better off with a more balanced approach. I don't mean to imply there are no topics that require serious consideration

Making a conscious choice to include laughter in your life will help you strike the appropriate balance and boost your morale at the same time.

11. List your assets and achievements.

Don't stage an elaborate episode of "This Is Your Life." Just take time periodically to list accomplishments so that you log them in. Many people, and you might be one of them, are very slow to appreciate their own achievements. Kept in proper perspective, a healthy consciousness of what you've accomplished and accumulated in terms of rewards over the years helps you to feel more confident about what you're capable of achieving today.

12. Talk to someone who always makes you feel good.

Preferably someone outside of your field. That might be your spouse, a close friend or family member, possibly a mentor. There is usually someone or several people in your life who have an uplifting effect on you. They're probably individuals with high self-esteem who respect and encourage you. Too many people are hesitant to ask for help. I know that has been one of my biggest problems over the years. The sooner you learn that asking for help with your morale is as important as asking for help on a project, the sooner your morale will improve.

13. Develop a hobby.

This might sound trite, but it's yet another way for you to expand your thinking. When your mental faculties are devoted to a narrow range of endeavors, you tend to quickly exhaust your capacity for thinking while wasting much of the broad range of interests your talents, knowledge and experiences will support. This doesn't mean carrying on multiple careers simultaneously. Your career path should be well-focused. But give other talents and abilities their moment in the sun to add new ways of sensing accomplishment.

When I first entered the speaking circuit I used to hit a hotel room after a long flight and lay wide awake. I couldn't put my mind on hold long enough to sleep. Everything I did was so narrowly focused that I began to lose focus. In the middle of a seminar, I couldn't remember what city I was in.

As soon as I took up collecting and reading old and rare books, my mental prowess changed dramatically. Initially, I resisted the notion of developing a hobby. But since I picked up a mental diversion, I can sleep more soundly, wake up more refreshed and be far more alert when I'm doing my lob. Now I spend my spare time in strange cities browsing through used bookstores and I spend much of my time on airplanes (I fly an average of 1,000 miles per day) reading what fascinating people have written.

14. Give help to someone who needs it.

There's no more effective way to climb out of your personal emotional rut than to get outside of yourself and help somebody else. Helping others in your working environment should always be a major priority. However, finding someone less fortunate than you (there are always people less fortunate than you) and giving them a hand on a regular basis (not just at holidays) helps to keep your life in perspective and exercises a nurturing side of your personality that's too easily ignored in your fast-paced world.

15. Make someone else happy.

This is different than helping someone else succeed or merely survive. It means spending just 10 minutes per day cheering people up. One person or several, it doesn't matter. If you make a concerted effort to cheer up someone else, you can't avoid boosting your own morale. It takes a surprisingly short time.

> *"There are some days when I think I'm going to die from an overdose of satisfaction."*
> —Salvador Dali

> *"Mirth is God's medicine; everybody ought to bathe
> in it. Contentment is the fountain of youth."*
> —Oliver Wendell Holmes

> *"I've found there is very little success where
> there is little laughter."*
> —Andrew Carnegie

> *"Wisdom is to know that rest is rust and that
> real life is in love, laughter, and work."*
> —Elbert Hubbard

What more can I say?

Your Personal Plan for Growth

"Every person has two educations; one which he receives from others and one, more importantly which he gives to himself [or herself]."

—Edward Gibbon

Jim Newton, Henry Ford, and Harvey Firestone stood staring up Madison Avenue through the large bay window of Firestone's apartment at the old Ritz Carlton in New York City. As the three men watched in silence, the streetlights went out. Section by section across town, the city fell dark. The glittering lights of Broadway were turned off and the torch on the Statue of Liberty blinked out.

It was the night of October 21, 1931, and all across the United States the lights were being switched off for two minutes to mark the death of Thomas Edison. Few mortal men had influenced life on Earth more positively than Edison had. In one lifetime, this prolific inventor had been granted 1,093 patents, one patent for every 10 to 12 days of his adult life.

Edison had invented *more* than 1,093 patented objects. He simply gave away his medical inventions in hopes they would be put into practice far and wide. As Henry Ford gazed out of Firestone's window at the darkening city that autumn night, he must have thought about how, as a young entrepreneur and visionary, Thomas Edison had taken the time to encourage him.

Jim Newton describes that evening as one of those breathtaking moments in life. I can't think of a better way to begin this final chapter on personal growth. The *high-performance process* is intended to increase your personal productivity. But why? Why invest so much in yourself and why stay with it for the rest of your life?

Inward focus for outward results

You must find what timeless contribution you can make to the human race and keep that contribution in sight at all times. Few people will ever affect life on this planet as profoundly as Thomas Edison. Some will—and maybe you're one of those people. But, even if you're not, timelessness should still be part of your plan for personal growth.

Elbert Hubbard said,

> *"We were not put here to keep things the same,*
> *but to make things better."*

That's a pretty straightforward philosophy. If what you're doing isn't making things better, then what are you doing it for? I'm not saying that you need to drop what you're doing and become Mother Teresa or devote your entire life to a high-profile humanitarian endeavor. But what you choose to do with your life, both professionally and personally, is either outward-focused or inward-focused.

Even if your outward focus doesn't extend beyond your spouse and family, it's still outside of *you.* As my wife and I rode on camels past the great Egyptian pyramids, I wondered if what I was doing was outward-focused. I wondered what monument, either physical or emotional, I would leave behind for my children and grandchildren: At the bottom line, your personal growth is tied to how outwardly focused you are.

This is not a bunch of motivational hype. This is your life. The issue of your personal growth and how profound your impact will be on the world around you only becomes irrelevant when it's blown out of perspective. The way you help make your organization a more pleasant and productive place to work is at stake more than whether someone will write your biography someday. So keep the issue of your personal growth in focus.

After reading everything in this book to this point, you're still in your moment of truth. You still need to make hard decisions and embark on new directions. The difference between you *now* and the way you were before you picked up this book is how much you know about your personal value in the scheme of things. You now know that the secret to becoming a high-performance person is to tap your own unique talents, knowledge and experience.

Hopefully, you're through trying to be what other people think you should be. The tool chest of methods and techniques I've now equipped you with only works on you. You can always use these tools to be more understanding and helpful to others, but you can't change anybody but you. That means *you're* the one on the hot seat.

What's in your hyphen?

A tombstone bears the date of when a life began and the date it ended. A simple hyphen stands for the rest of it. You can look at the *high-performance process* as a way to pack more into your hyphen. Years from now, how will you be remembered? What you choose to do today has everything to do with what will be said about you in the years to come.

Figure 7. 1 illustrates what happens during your hyphen, depending upon the choices you make. The curving lines influence each other as time passes. For example, the *health and well-being* line absolutely begins at birth and ends at death. However, your goals line will either hasten your demise or prolong your life. As the goals line descends, initiative and desire fall off, too.

When initiative and desire fall off, your health and well-being tend to disintegrate. The faster your initiative and desire fall off, the more rapidly your health and well-being decline. In the United States, the average time between retirement and death is only a few years. Retirement for many is so short that some insurance experts recommend that, after retirement, you might as well go lay in the box and wait. L.L. Taylor wrote:

"When you get that gold watch after 35 years of dedicated service, take that gold watch and drive directly to the undertaker. You've got just enough time to make a down payment."

Personal Growth's "Moment of Truth"

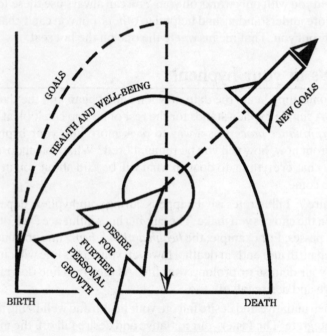

Figure 7.1

The difference between work being a goal in itself and goals being a reflection of your desired rewards is personal choice. Either you make your own goals or someone else will make them for you. I watched a 78-year-old executive give a talk a few years ago. Few people are as full of life at any age as this man was at 78. What he said really rang my bell.

His message was that, when you hit the age of 50, you don't make shorter plans, you make *longer* plans. He went on to say that if you have no further goals, you're telling your body that it's all right to begin the death process. Make no mistake about it, *death is a process.* Unlike the *high-performance process* that requires focus and effort on your part, death will slowly and insidiously overtake you if you have no goals leading you away from it.

As the illustration indicates, a powerful force called *desire for further personal growth* can enter the picture and make that rapidly deteriorating goals curve take off again. It can happen at most any time. As long as you're not in the ground yet, a renewed desire for further personal growth can revive you. The earlier in your life you commit to personal growth, the more fulfilled years you will enjoy.

As the saying goes, youth is wasted on the young. Unless you know the value of strength and energy, you'll probably waste it. When the force of your desire for further personal growth bangs up against the descending goals line, the goals line takes off again, often faster, higher, stronger, and farther than it's ever gone. The older you are, the more dramatic the change.

Colonel Sanders didn't begin his fried chicken empire until he was 65 years old. George Burns had a career comeback like few have ever seen, winning his first Academy Award in his 80s. Years ago, Burns spoke to a college audience and a young person asked him what the secret to great acting was. Without a second thought, Burns shot back, "Honesty. If you can fake that, you've got it made."

Despite his age, Burns was getting faster, not slower. Another student asked him if he ever worried about dying. Without hesitation, Burns replied, "I'm booked." He was too busy looking ahead at his upcoming engagements to worry about anything as unproductive as death. Jim Newton, who had the close friendships with the great men I've previously mentioned, had to start over from scratch at the age of 68.

He had endured a financial collapse but resolved that he wasn't going to quit. How many people do you know who will refuse to quit in their late 60s? How many people do you know who quit long before that? Newton was so broke, he set up a desk in the lobby of a Florida hotel where he was living and published the number of the lobby pay telephone as his business number. Ten years later, his company had 15 offices going full force. He was nearly 80 when he sold his company for a substantial sum.

After he sold his company, I asked Jim Newton if he might retire. The man bubbled over with energy as he told me that his greatest work is still in front of him. How's that for an attitude? My wife and I still spend time with Ellie Newton (now 102 years young), recalling her husband's vigor and enthusiasm. Jim Newton was 20 years old when he was building Edison park in Fort Myers, Florida. A lifetime later, Newton has contributed to the health and well-being of all those who knew him more than ever.

More questions

As a good mentor, it's incumbent upon me to stimulate your thinking. That's what Jim Newton has done for me. It was on a trip to Florida to visit Jim that my wife and I formulated these last questions to help you focus on your further personal growth:

1. If you could spend 10 days alone asking questions of 10 great people, living or dead (one person per day), who would they be?

    Heroes can be great historical figures or anyone from whom you can learn—it's up to you. The reason you feel you can learn something from the people you list is because you sense your strengths and beliefs somehow line up with theirs.

2. If you could spend 10 days alone asking questions of people who are living only (no duplications from the first list), which 10 would you pick?

These questions reveal who your living heroes are. You now have a list of 20 guideposts for your customized training program.

3. In one sentence, which facets of each listed person's personality or accomplishments do you find most attractive?

    For example, I put Winston Churchill on my list because he had a gift and passion for oratory. He was not only a great thinker and writer, he was a master at inspiring an audience with his words. (The fact that he flunked English as a schoolboy is an interesting aside.) This list helps you focus your training from these great people's lives.

4. Why would any one of these 20 people enjoy spending a day in isolation with you?

    My wife answered the last question brilliantly. She said since she didn't know who her listed people's best friends were (or are), there was no reason she couldn't feel comfortable imagining herself as their best friend. Fame was not a requirement to be their friend. Furthermore, she felt they would enjoy spending a day with her because she is so anxious to learn—*about them.*

5. If you were given 28 hours per day for the rest of your life instead of the 24 you now have, what would you do with the four extra hours?

I gave these questions to another friend of mine, Og Mandino. Og is the author of the best seller, *The Greatest Salesman In the World,* and a great thinker in his own right. After studying the questions, he immediately commented on how the answers speak volumes about your personal values. Your personal values are the lifeblood of your personality as defined by your natural talents, knowledge and experience.

How else are you going to discover, cultivate, and stay true to your uniqueness as a human being if you don't have a fix on your personal value barometer? How better to explain why trying to be what others want you to be is such a frustrating and ultimately futile effort. As the character Felix said in the Neil Simon play, *The Odd Couple,* "We are who we are."

Can we get better? Of course, but the goal is not to pretend you're someone other than yourself, but to get better at discovering and developing your own personal strengths. These final questions will serve you as a navigational device if you take a few moments to answer them honestly and thoughtfully. Then use what you learn as you work through the *high-performance process.*

The first two questions provide you with a path for your own learning by focusing on who represents the most admirable and attractive components of human behavior. Question three specifies what you value most about each person. The fourth question speaks directly to your sense of self-value as you relate to the people you listed. Finally, question five exposes how you value your time resources.

Incidentally, the time-planning component of the *high-performance process* can open up four or more extra hours per day through more efficient time-use habits. You can't get away with saying that you could accomplish great things if only you had a few more hours in the day. Great football and basketball coaches don't say there wasn't enough time to win the game when the final gun or buzzer cuts short the big come-from-behind rally. More effective use of regulation time would have made the difference between victory and defeat.

And so...

I want you to use the *high-performance process* to be the best you can possibly be. That way you'll always know you did the best you possibly could for yourself and everyone around you. It's safer to have an enemy, confident in his or her true identity than to have a friend who doesn't know who s/he is. Never approach a bull from the front, a horse from the rear or a fool from any direction and always ride on the high side when the folks around you refuse to declare their intentions.

As your potential turns to performance on the pathway to power, always remember this:

Seize the Day! The best is on its way!

For more information on Danny Cox's speaking programs (live or recorded) contact:

Danny Cox
Acceleration Unlimited
17381 Bonner Drive, Suite 101
Tustin, California 92780
714-838-3030
http:*www.dannycox.com*
E-mail: MACH175@aol.com

Index

About the Author

Danny Cox flew supersonic fighters for the U.S. Air Force for 10 years. He has served as a test pilot and air show pilot. After leaving the Air force, he joined a nationally known sales company, moving from salesperson to first vice president in five years. Using the leadership and motivational skills he developed, his district increased sales 800 percent in those years.He is a member of the National Speakers' Association Hall of fame—an honor shared by others such as Dr. Norman Vincent Peale and Zig Ziglar. He is also a member of the prestigious 20-member Speakers' Round Table. He is based in Tustin, California.

John Hoover, previously a manager with Walt Disney Company as well as McGraw-Hill, is an entrepreneur who writes, produces, and directs entertainment, educational, and corporate training, development, and sales programs for corporate clients. He lives in Southern California.

The authors' previous book, *Leadership When the Heat is On* (1992), is in its 12th printing.

For more information on Danny Cox's speaking programs (live or recorded) contact:

Danny Cox   714-838-3030
Acceleration Unlimited   http:www.dannycox.com
17381 Bonner Drive, Suite 101   E-mail: MACH175@aol.com
Tustin,California 92780